The Lewis and Clark Expedition

Recent Titles in
Greenwood Guides to Historic Events, 1500–1900

The Dreyfus Affair
Leslie Derfler

The War of 1812
David S. Heidler and Jeanne T. Heidler

The Atlantic Slave Trade
Johannes Postma

Manifest Destiny
David S. Heidler and Jeanne T. Heidler

American Railroads in the Nineteenth Century
Augustus J. Veenendaal

Reconstruction
Claudine L. Ferrell

The Spanish-American War
Kenneth E. Hendrickson, Jr.

The American Revolution
Joseph C. Morton

The French Revolution
Linda S. Frey and Marsha L. Frey

The French and Indian War
Alfred A. Cave

The Lewis and Clark Expedition

HARRY WILLIAM FRITZ

Greenwood Guides to Historic Events, 1500–1900
Linda S. Frey and Marsha L. Frey, Series Editors

GREENWOOD PRESS
Westport, Connecticut • London

Library of Congress Cataloging-in-Publication Data

Fritz, Harry W., 1937–
    The Lewis and Clark Expedition / Harry William Fritz.
        p. cm. — (Greenwood guides to historic events, 1500–1900, ISSN 1538–442X)
    Includes bibliographical references and index.
    ISBN 0–313–31661–9 (alk. paper)
    1. Lewis and Clark Expedition (1804–1806) I. Title. II. Series.
F592.7.F75   2004
917.8—dc22   2003026704

British Library Cataloguing in Publication Data is available.

Library of Congress Catalog Card Number: 2003026704
ISBN: 0–313–31661–9
ISSN: 1538–442X

First published in 2004

Greenwood Press, 88 Post Road West, Westport, CT 06881
An imprint of Greenwood Publishing Group, Inc.
www.greenwood.com

Printed in the United States of America

∞™

The paper used in this book complies with the
Permanent Paper Standard issued by the National
Information Standards Organization (Z39.48–1984).

10   9   8   7   6   5   4   3   2   1

CONTENTS

Photo essay follows Chapter 6.

SERIES FOREWORD

American statesman Adlai Stevenson stated that "We can chart our future clearly and wisely only when we know the path which has led to the present." This series, Greenwood Guides to Historic Events, 1500–1900, is designed to illuminate that path by focusing on events from 1500 to 1900 that have shaped the world. The years 1500 to 1900 include what historians call the Early Modern Period (1500 to 1789, the onset of the French Revolution) and part of the modern period (1789 to 1900).

In 1500, an acceleration of key trends marked the beginnings of an interdependent world and the posting of seminal questions that changed the nature and terms of intellectual debate. The series closes with 1900, the inauguration of the twentieth century. This period witnessed profound economic, social, political, cultural, religious, and military changes. An industrial and technological revolution transformed the modes of production, marked the transition from a rural to an urban economy, and ultimately raised the standard of living. Social classes and distinctions shifted. The emergence of the territorial and later the national state altered man's relations with and view of political authority. The shattering of the religious unity of the Roman Catholic world in Europe marked the rise of a new pluralism. Military revolutions changed the nature of warfare. The books in this series emphasize the complexity and diversity of the human tapestry and include political, economic, social, intellectual, military, and cultural topics. Some of the authors focus on events in U.S. history such as the Salem Witchcraft Trials, the American Revolution, the abolitionist movement, and the Civil War. Others analyze European topics, such as the Reformation and Counter

Reformation and the French Revolution. Still others bridge cultures and continents by examining the voyages of discover, the Atlantic slave trade, and the Age of Imperialism. Some focus on intellectual questions that have shaped the modern world, such as Darwin's *Origin of Species* or on turning points such as the Age of Romanticism. Others examine defining economic, religious, or legal events or issues such as the building of the railroads, the Second Great Awakening, and abolitionism. Heroes (e.g., Lewis and Clark), scientists (e.g., Darwin), military leaders (e.g., Napoleon), poets (e.g., Byron), stride across its pages. Many of these events were seminal in that they marked profound changes or turning points. The Scientific Revolution, for example, changed the way individuals viewed themselves and their world.

The authors, acknowledged experts in their fields, synthesize key events, set developments within the larger historical context, and, most important, present a well-balanced, well-written account that integrates the most recent scholarship in the field.

The topics were chosen by an advisory board composed of historians, high school history teachers, and school librarians to support the curriculum and meet student research needs. The volumes are designed to serve as resources for student research and to provide clearly written interpretations of topics central to the secondary school and lower-level undergraduate history curriculum. Each author outlines a basic chronology to guide the reader through often confusing events and a historical overview to set those events within a narrative framework. Three to five topical chapters underscore critical aspects of the event. In the final chapter the author examines the impact and consequences of the event. Biographical sketches furnish background on the lives and contributions of the players who strut across this stage. Ten to fifteen primary documents ranging from letters to diary entries, song lyrics, proclamations, and posters, cast light on the event, provide material for student essays, and stimulate a critical engagement with the sources. Introductions identify the authors of the documents and the main issues. In some cases a glossary of selected terms is provided as a guide to the reader. Each work contains an annotated bibliography of recommended books, articles, CD-ROMs, Internet sites, videos, and films that set the materials within the historical debate.

These works will lead to a more sophisticated understanding of the events and debates that have shaped the modern world and will stimulate a more active engagement with the issues that still affect us. It has been a particularly enriching experience to work closely with such dedicated professionals. We have come to know and value even more highly the authors in this series and our editors at Greenwood, particularly Kevin Ohe. In many cases they have become more than colleagues; they have become friends. To them and to future historians we dedicate this series.

Linda S. Frey
University of Montana

Marsha L. Frey
Kansas State University

PREFACE

At this writing the nation is celebrating the bicentennial anniversary of the Lewis and Clark Expedition of 1803–1806. Interest in the Expedition has never been higher. The complete records of Lewis and Clark and their men have recently been published in a magnificent 13-volume edition, now appearing in paperback. Ken Burns's and Dayton Duncan's four-hour PBS special thrilled the general public. Their illustrated history of "The Journey of the Corps of Discovery" graced coffee tables across the land. Stephen Ambrose's exciting biography of Meriwether Lewis, *Undaunted Courage,* introduced the Expedition to hundreds of thousands of new enthusiasts. Literally millions of people will follow the Lewis and Clark Trail and visit historic sites associated with the Expedition. Lewis and Clark are alive and well in modern America.

The Expedition has always fascinated students because of the geographical secrets it revealed. Lewis and Clark went up the Missouri River beyond any point previously reached by Europeans and were the first Americans to confront the awesome escarpments of the Rocky Mountains. Their crossing of the Rockies in search of the fabled Northwest Passage is at the heart of their experience.

For many years, all that was known about the Expedition concerned its route. In the twentieth century, the original journals of Lewis and Clark were at last published. They contained a storehouse of biological, ethnological, and scientific information, which has enhanced the reputation of Lewis and Clark as naturalists. In recent years attention has shifted to the many peoples encountered by Lewis and Clark on their western journey. Some three dozen Native American tribes, most still unknown, provided sustenance and guidance along the way.

Without this Indian assistance, the Lewis and Clark Expedition would not have succeeded. We now ask, not what the explorers thought of Indians, but how Indian people reacted to Lewis and Clark.

This book is not designed to answer all questions about Lewis and Clark. The bibliography lists far more comprehensive accounts, including documents, letters, biographies, and scientific analyses. This is an introduction, expected to raise as many issues as it resolves. It consists of a chronology or timeline of the Expedition, a brief narrative account, biographical sketches of the principals, a few documents, a key to unusual terms, and an annotated bibliography. It is only the first step on an expedition of your own.

NB—All quotations in this book are transcribed as originally written, with all the peculiarities and eccentricities of early American spelling and grammar. The reader is thus introduced to the flavor of the times and of the writers. There are no [*sic*]s.

CHRONOLOGY OF EVENTS

April 13, 1743	Thomas Jefferson born at Shadwell, Albemarle County, Virginia.
August 1, 1770	William Clark born in Caroline County, Virginia.
August 18, 1774	Meriwether Lewis born in Albemarle County, Virginia.
May 11, 1792	Captain Robert Gray discovers the mouth of the Columbia River and names the river after his ship, the *Columbia Rediviva*.
October 1, 1800	Spain cedes Louisiana to France in the secret Treaty of San Ildefonso.
February 17, 1801	Thomas Jefferson becomes the third president of the United States by vote of the House of Representatives.
January 18, 1803	Thomas Jefferson's secret message to Congress requests financial support for a western expedition.
May 2, 1803	James Monroe and Robert Livingston sign a treaty in Paris transferring Louisiana to the United States for $15 million.
July 5, 1803	Meriwether Lewis leaves Washington, D.C., en route to the Pacific Ocean.
July 6–9, 1803	Lewis assembles the party's weaponry at Harpers Ferry, Virginia.
July 15–August 29, 1803	Lewis oversees the construction of his keelboat in Pittsburgh, Pennsylvania.
August 31, 1803	Meriwether Lewis sets out from Pittsburgh down the Ohio River.

August 31–November 14, 1803	Meriwether Lewis's Ohio River itinerary: Wheeling (September 1–9), Marietta (September 13), Cincinnati (September 28–October 4), Louisville (October 15–26), Fort Massac (November 11–13).
October 15–26, 1803	Meriwether Lewis and William Clark join forces at Louisville, Kentucky.
October 20, 1803	The United States Senate ratifies the Louisiana Purchase by a vote of 24 to 7.
November 14–20, 1803	At the confluence of the Ohio and Mississippi Rivers.
November 20–December 12, 1803	Ascending the Mississippi River.
December 13, 1803	William Clark puts his men into the Wood River Camp (Camp Dubois), in Illinois opposite the mouth of the Missouri River.
December 13, 1803–May 14, 1804	Wintering at Camp Dubois.
December 20, 1803	In New Orleans, the United States takes formal possession of Louisiana from France.
March 9–10, 1804	In St. Louis, the Louisiana Territory passes from Spain to France to the United States.
May 14, 1804	William Clark embarks "under a jentle brease" up the Missouri River.
May 16–21, 1804	At St. Charles.
June 26–29, 1804	At the mouth of the Kansas River.
July 21, 1804	At the mouth of the Platte River.
July 22–27, 1804	At Camp White Catfish.
July 30–August 3, 1804	At Council Bluffs, Iowa, with the Oto and Missouri Indians.
August 20, 1804	Sergeant Charles Floyd dies near Sioux City, Iowa, presumably of a ruptured appendix—the only fatality suffered by the Corps of Discovery.
August 22, 1804	Patrick Gass elected Sergeant.
August 24–25, 1804	At the White Stone (Vermillion) River, and Spirit Mound.

August 27–30, 1804	At the James River, with the Yankton Sioux.
September 24–28, 1804	At the Bad River, with the Teton Sioux.
October 8–12, 1804	Near the Grand River, with the Arikara Indians.
October 26, 1804– April 7, 1805	With the Mandan and Hidatsa Indians near the mouth of the Knife River.
February 11, 1805	Jean Baptiste born to Toussaint Charbonneau and Sacagawea.
April 7, 1805	"This little fleet" of six small canoes and two large pirogues departs Fort Mandan for the Pacific.
April 12, 1805	At the mouth of the Little Missouri River.
April 25–28, 1805	At the mouth of the Yellowstone River, Clark's "Roche johne."
May 3, 1805	At the mouth of the Poplar River.
May 8, 1805	At the mouth of the Milk River, "the river which scoalds at all others."
May 20, 1805	At the mouth of the Musselshell River.
May 29, 1805	At the mouth of the Judith River.
June 2–12, 1805	At the mouth of the Marias River.
June 13, 1805	Meriwether Lewis "discovers" the Great Falls of the Missouri, "this truly magnifficent and sublimely grand object."
June 15–July 14, 1805	At the Great Falls of the Missouri.
June 21–July 2, 1805	Portaging around the Great Falls.
July 19, 1805	At "the gates of the rocky mountains," "the most remarkable clifts that we have yet seen."
July 25–29, 1805	At the Three Forks of the Missouri—the Gallatin, Madison, and Jefferson Rivers—"an essential point in the geography of this western part of the Continent."
August 12, 1805	Meriwether Lewis leaves America—he crosses the Continental Divide at Lemhi Pass and "first tasted the water of the great Columbia river."
August 13–30, 1805	With the Shoshoni Indians, in Idaho and Montana.

September 4–6, 1805	With the Flathead Indians on the East Fork of the Bitterroot River.
September 9–11, 1805	At "Travellers rest," near the mouth of Lolo Creek.
September 11–22, 1805	Crossing the Bitterroot Mountains, over Lolo Pass.
September 20–25, 1805	With the Nez Perce Indians on the Weippe Prairie.
September 26–October 7, 1805	At "Canoe Camp" on the Clearwater River.
October 10, 1805	At the confluence of the Clearwater and Snake Rivers.
October 16–18, 1805	At the confluence of the Snake and Columbia Rivers.
October 18–19, 1805	With Chief Yelleppit and the Walla Walla Indians.
October 19, 1805	At the mouth of the Umatilla River.
October 21, 1805	At the mouth of the John Day River.
October 22, 1805	Passed the mouth of the Deschutes River.
October 22–28, 1805	At Celilo Falls and The Dalles of the Columbia River.
October 30–November 2, 1805	At the Cascades of the Columbia River.
November 2, 1805	Through the Columbia River Gorge.
November 6, 1805	At the mouth of the Cowlitz River.
November 7, 1805	"Ocian in view! O! the joy." It's not the Pacific Ocean, only the estuary of the Columbia River.
November 8–26, 1805	On the north shore of the Columbia River estuary.
November 26, 1805	The party crosses the Columbia River.
November 26–December 6, 1805	On the south shore of the Columbia River estuary.
December 3, 1805	"William Clark December 3rd 1805. By Land from the U. States in 1804 & 1805."

December 7–24, 1805	Building Fort Clatsop. Most of the men moved in on the 24th. "The fort was completed" on December 30.
December 8–10, 1805	William Clark on a scouting expedition to Seaside.
December 25, 1805– March 23, 1806	At Fort Clatsop.
December 28, 1805– February 21, 1806	Saltmaking at Seaside.
January 6–10, 1806	Clark's expedition to a beached whale on Ecola Creek, south of Tillamook Head.
March 23, 1806	The Lewis and Clark Expedition departs Fort Clatsop and ascends the Columbia River.
March 31–April 5, 1806	At the mouth of the Sandy River. Clark explores the Willamette.
April 9–12, 1806	At the Cascades of the Columbia River.
April 15–21, 1806	At The Dalles and Celilo Falls.
April 27–30, 1806	With Chief Yelleppit at the mouth of the Walla Walla River.
April 30–May 5, 1806	The Expedition leaves the Columbia River on an overland trek to the Clearwater.
May 5–13, 1806	On the Clearwater River en route to the Nez Perce encampment near Kamiah.
May 14–June 10, 1806	At Camp Chopunnish with the Nez Perce Indians.
May 27–June 2, 1806	Sergeant John Ordway's trip to the Salmon and Snake Rivers for fish, with Fraser and Weiser.
June 10–14, 1806	On the Weippe Prairie.
June 15–21, 1806	False start into the Bitterroot Mountains; still too much snow.
June 22–24, 1806	Back on the Weippe Prairie.
June 24–30, 1806	Crossing the Bitterroot Mountains over Lolo Pass.
June 30–July 3, 1806	At "Travellers rest."

March 3, 1807	Meriwether Lewis appointed governor of Louisiana.
October 11, 1809	Meriwether Lewis dies of self-inflicted wounds at Grinder's Stand on the Natchez Trace in Tennessee.
July 4, 1826	Thomas Jefferson dies at Monticello.
September 1, 1838	William Clark dies of natural causes in St. Louis.

CHAPTER 1

PROLOGUE

The chronology is straightforward and simple. Thomas Jefferson became President of the United States in 1801. He hired Meriwether Lewis, a bachelor, and gave him a room in the White House. When Jefferson bought Louisiana from France in 1803, his expedition commander was at hand. He sent Lewis and another army officer, William Clark, up the Missouri River in 1804, to explore the Louisiana Territory and find a water route to the Pacific. Lewis and Clark accomplished both tasks and opened the West to American expansion.

All this is true, after a fashion. But the real story, like all history, is more complicated and therefore more fascinating. Jefferson almost lost the presidency. He tied in electoral votes with Aaron Burr, and the election was decided in the House of Representatives. It took the House 36 ballots to choose Jefferson over Burr. The nation came within two weeks of Inauguration Day (March 4, 1801) without a constitutional leader.[1] Meriwether Lewis went to work for Jefferson, but as a "secretary"—an administrative assistant similar to a modern military liaison or aide-de-camp. When, sometime late in 1802, Jefferson decided to explore the Missouri drainage, he announced no commander. Indeed, the territory still belonged to France. Jefferson would send an American expedition into foreign country. If we believe him, Lewis had to ask for the job as commander. Instead of a water route across the continent, Lewis and Clark discovered the Rocky Mountains. The land was not theirs to open; it was inhabited by native peoples from St. Louis to the ocean. The Lewis and Clark Expedition (1803–1806), highly successful in many ways, had little immediate impact upon American destiny.

The expedition was the product of complex international diplomatic and economic factors. But historical events do not just happen.

People make history. In 1802 President Thomas Jefferson took advantage of the events of his times and made the Lewis and Clark Expedition happen.[2]

On May 12, 1792, Captain Robert Gray, a trader operating from Boston, piloted his vessel across a treacherous bar on the Pacific northwest coast of America and found himself in the estuary of a mighty river flowing from the east. He named the river after his ship, the *Columbia.* In the following year Alexander Mackenzie, a Scotsman working for the British North West Company deep in the interior of Canada, crossed the headwaters of a river he thought might reach the coast. It is a measure of European geographical ignorance that it took fifteen years, until 1807, to realize that Gray and Mackenzie were on the same river.

Mackenzie, who had already, in 1789, traveled down a swift river to the Arctic Ocean, became in 1793 the first European to cross the North American continent north of Mexico. The fur trader envisioned a lucrative British economic monopoly in the entire Columbia drainage. Already a thriving China trade in sea-otter skins was underway. Mackenzie's exploits were little known in the 1790s, but in 1801 he published an account of his escapades, *Voyages from Montreal.* Jefferson read the book in 1802, and alarms sounded. The United States was in danger of surrendering the Pacific Northwest without a fight.

Louisiana has a complicated history. France originally claimed the entire Mississippi Valley, based on the journey by Sieur Robert Cavelier de La Salle down the river to its mouth in 1682. Spain claimed the land along the Gulf Coast and called it Florida. In the middle, on the east bank of the Mississippi but technically an island, was the largest French settlement in Louisiana, the Isle d'Orleans, or New Orleans. Another river town, St. Louis, was founded in 1764.

In 1761, during the Seven Years' War (the French and Indian War in America), Spain made the ill-advised decision to ally with France against Great Britain. The lure was the island of Minorca in the Mediterranean and also, in a secret treaty in 1762, New Orleans and all Louisiana west of the Mississippi River. Spain quickly lost the prime seaports and trading posts of Havana, in Cuba, and Manila, in the Philippines, to the British fleet. In the Peace of Paris in 1763, which ended the war, Spain traded Florida to Britain for the return of Havana and Manila, and it retained Louisiana, now defined loosely as all western drainages of the Mississippi River. The British divided Florida into east and west provinces, the border set variously at the Apalachicola, Perdido, and Pearl Rivers.

In another Peace of Paris in 1783, which ended the War of American Independence, Spain reacquired the Floridas from Britain. The Spanish controlled the "right of deposit" at New Orleans—the right of American farmers to float goods down the Mississippi and unload them in the city. This was a contentious issue between the United States and Spain after the Revolution, until resolved in America's favor by Pinckney's Treaty of 1795. America's role in world affairs shifted dramatically in the fall of 1800. On September 30 the United States and France signed the Convention of Mortfontaine, an agreement ending four years of undeclared naval warfare and settling accounts. But the very next day, October 1, in the secret Treaty of San Ildefonso, Napoleonic France reacquired Louisiana from Spain. Spain received Italian territory, the Kingdom of Etruria, to be ruled by the Prince of Parma, the son-in-law of Charles IV of Spain. Napoleon promised never again to alienate Louisiana.[3]

On day one, the United States and France proclaimed peace on the Atlantic Ocean. On day two, France, the most powerful nation on earth, came into possession of America's thousand-mile western frontier.

France now owned Louisiana, but it never occupied it. Spanish administrators continued to govern the province. Late in 1802, Spain violated Pinckney's Treaty and removed the right of deposit, closing the Mississippi River to free American commerce. Although Spain restored the right in March 1803, Thomas Jefferson had already acted.

Rumors of the Louisiana retrocession filtered into the United States in 1801; the transaction was confirmed in 1802. Jefferson was nervous. He felt threatened. The British threatened to create an economic bastion in the Northwest, the French threatened to block American expansion across the Mississippi, and the Spanish threatened to close vital American commerce on the river.

"There is on the globe one single spot, the possessor of which is our natural and habitual enemy," Jefferson wrote to Robert Livingston, the U.S. minister to France. "It is New Orleans."[4] The president spoke belligerently, but behind the scenes he worked to secure America's interests. Perhaps France would sell New Orleans? Jefferson asked Congress for $2 million to buy the city.

Napoleon toyed with reestablishing the French empire in North America, which had been lost in 1763. Louisiana would be a giant supply depot and granary for a French army in the Caribbean, poised to retake Saint Domingue from slave rebels. But the rebels (and yellow fever) decimated the French forces. War with Great Britain loomed. Louisiana became expendable.

Ironically, the first hard evidence we have of Jefferson's western intentions comes in a letter from the Spanish minister in Washington to his home government. On December 2, 1802, Carlos Martinez de Yrujo reported a conversation "the other day" with Jefferson, in which the president inquired about sending "a group of travelers" up the Missouri River for "the advancement of geography."[5] Jefferson had no intention of stopping at the Continental Divide (the western border of Louisiana) but would proceed to the Pacific. At that moment, not one square inch of the country that Lewis and Clark would later traverse was owned by the United States.

Thus, a fortuitous combination of events impelled Jefferson to act: Mackenzie's book, Spanish duplicity, French posturing. These seeds found fertile ground in the president's mind. On three previous occasions he had tried to interest an explorer in the American West.[6] Two decades earlier he had approached George Rogers Clark, the Virginia hero of the American Revolution and William's older brother. In Paris in 1785 he spoke with John Ledyard, who had sailed with James Cook to the northwest coast in the 1770s. Ledyard planned to travel through Russia, cross the Bering Sea, and hike across America west to east. He got as far as Irkutsk in Siberia. André Michaux was a French botanist who wanted to pick flowers from Philadelphia to the Pacific in 1793. He foundered in Kentucky. In all these instances Jefferson sought to take advantage of someone else's aspirations. He could beseech but not command. Now, however, in 1802, he was in charge. He was the President of the United States, and anything was possible.

All the pieces now came together. Though Spain demurred, Jefferson pressed on. He always considered the Spanish empire in America as overripe fruit, soon to fall to the United States. He found his commander, Meriwether Lewis, working by his side in the executive mansion. Lewis was undoubtedly the "intelligent officer" Jefferson had in mind when he informed Congress of his plans on January 18, 1803. At the end of February the president boasted of Lewis's capabilities to several correspondents. "It was impossible to find a character who to a compleat science in botany, natural history, mineralogy & astronomy," he admitted, "joined the firmness of constitution & character, prudence, habits adapted to the woods, & a familiarity with the Indian manners & character, requisite for this undertaking. All the latter qualifications Capt. Lewis has."[7]

France provided the stunner. Jefferson wanted to buy New Orleans; Napoleon offered all Louisiana—a land so vast as to be almost incomprehensible. Livingston, floored by the offer, claimed lack of authority to accept, but James Monroe showed up in Paris and closed the deal. On May 2, 1803, France sold Louisiana, all 828,000 square miles of it, to the United States, for $15 million. Lewis and Clark would indeed explore Upper Louisiana. Their expedition would take place on American soil—until they reached the Continental Divide.

The United States claimed, with some justification, that West Florida was part of Louisiana. Spain said no. But Spanish control was weak, and in 1810 President James Madison proclaimed American occupancy of Florida west of the Pearl River. Two years later the U.S. formally annexed West Florida, attached part of it to Louisiana, and admitted the State of Louisiana to the Union. Spain sold East Florida (the present state) to the United States in 1819.

Two weeks before Lewis left Washington, Jefferson set down in writing his expectations of success. "The object of your mission," he stated forthrightly, "is to explore the Missouri river, & such principal stream of it, as, by its course and communication with the waters of the Pacific ocean, whether the Columbia, Oregan, Colorado or any other river may offer the most direct & practicable water communication across this continent for the purposes of commerce."[8] The president demanded careful observation, measurements, and records, especially of the expected portage between Missouri and Columbia waters. He was interested in Indians, soils, animals, minerals, and climate. Believing, as all geographers did, that the great rivers of the West originated on the same "height of land," he thought the headwaters of the Missouri adjoined the Rio Grande and Colorado. His expedition had geopolitical potential. Thus he was quite concerned about the safety of his emissaries and their papers. Jefferson's instructions provide a comprehensive model for all future exploration.

The expedition Jefferson planned, although described as literary and scientific, would necessarily be military in nature, for several reasons. The United States would enter dangerous international waters.

French troops might occupy Louisiana; the British might mobilize; the Spanish might interfere. (Spain feared that discovery of the headwaters of the Missouri would place America uncomfortably close to Santa Fe. Three Spanish armies would set out to intercept Lewis and Clark.) Cost was a factor—army personnel came cheap, were available at forts and posts, and could be disciplined. Indians might be hostile. And Meriwether Lewis, the default commander, was a U.S. Army captain.

Notes

1. The best single-volume biography of Thomas Jefferson is Noble E. Cunningham, Jr., *In Pursuit of Reason: The Life of Thomas Jefferson* (Baton Rouge: Louisiana State University Press, 1987). The most recent account of the critical election of 1800 is Bernard A. Weisberger, *America Afire: Jefferson, Adams, and the Revolutionary Election of 1800* (New York: William Morrow, 2000).

2. The best general history of the Lewis and Clark Expedition is David Lavender, *The Way to the Western Sea: Lewis and Clark across the Continent* (New York: Harper & Row, 1988).

3. The best general account of the complicated Louisiana Purchase is Marshall Sprague, *So Vast, So Beautiful a Land: Louisiana and the Purchase* (Boston: Little, Brown, 1974).

4. Jefferson to Robert R. Livingston, 18 April 1802, *The Portable Thomas Jefferson*, ed. Merrill D. Peterson (New York: Viking Press, 1975), 485–88.

5. Carlos Martinez de Yrujo to Pedro Cevallos, 2 December 1802, *Letters of the Lewis and Clark Expedition, with Related Documents, 1783–1854*, ed. Donald Jackson, 2 vols. (Urbana: University of Illinois Press, 1978), I, 4–7.

6. On Jefferson and the West, see Donald D. Jackson, *Thomas Jefferson and the Stony Mountains: Exploring the West from Monticello* (Urbana: University of Illinois Press, 1981). See also James P. Ronda, *Jefferson's West: A Journey with Lewis and Clark* (Monticello: Thomas Jefferson Foundation, 2000).

7. Jefferson to Benjamin Smith Barton, 27 February 1803, *Letters*, I, 16–17.

8. Jefferson's Instructions to Lewis, 20 June 1803, *Letters*, I, 61–66.

CHAPTER 2

THROUGH THE MANDAN WINTER

The Lewis and Clark Expedition was a transcontinental trek—from Washington, D.C., to the Pacific and back. Meriwether Lewis left the nation's capital on July 5, 1803. He arrived back in town on December 28, 1806—1,273 days later. The Expedition began and ended at the White House.

Lewis first traveled to Harpers Ferry, the federal arsenal about fifty miles from Washington, where the Shenandoah River flows into the Potomac. He collected his order of 15 model 1803 short-barreled, .54-caliber flintlock muskets. This low number indicates that even at this late date he anticipated a small, tightly knit group, on the order of the President's suggested 10 or 12 men.

Lewis had designed the framework for an "iron boat"—the skeleton of a 30-foot canoe he would carry up the river until it was time to assemble it, cut wooden struts and seats, and cover it with animal hides. He arranged for it and other items to be shipped to Pittsburgh.

At Pittsburgh, Lewis's optimistic timetable for 1803 unraveled. He had hoped to be two or three hundred miles up the Missouri River by winter. But the keelboat he had ordered was not yet ready. This river craft would carry most of his supplies and equipment. It was big—55 feet long, 8 feet wide at the beam, with a 31-foot hold and a cabin at the stern. The owner of the shipyard, an alcoholic, had problems keeping a trained crew on task. A few days turned into six weeks; it was almost September when the keelboat finally struck the Ohio River. Unfortunately, it had been a dry year, and late in the season the water level was just six inches in places. The keelboat drew three feet. Lewis and his men spent a good deal of time rocking and pushing the boat over gravel shoals and sandbars. On numerous occasions they admitted defeat, and Lewis was forced to hire a team of horses or oxen from local farmers to drag the boat over the high spots.

The first hundred miles (to Wheeling) were the worst. After that the Ohio's tributaries lifted the water level sufficiently so that he hired help only twice. Past Marietta he floated to Cincinnati, where he stopped for a few days to examine mastodon bones at nearby Big Bend Lick. In the middle of October he reached the Falls of the Ohio and the twin cities of Louisville, Kentucky, and Clarksville, Indiana. William Clark was there, living in Clarksville with his brother George Rogers Clark. The two old friends and army compatriots met for the first time since 1796. Clark had recruited nine young men from Kentucky; they all became members of the permanent party. The Lewis and Clark Expedition was taking shape.

The Falls of the Ohio are no more—they have long since been locked and canalized. But in 1803 it was a heady adventure to run the rapids for two miles, dropping 24 feet. Lewis hired an experienced river pilot, and the keelboat survived. Still to come were the Great Falls of the Missouri, and the Cascades of the Columbia. The Ohio was a harbinger.

The enlarged party floated on down the Ohio, to its confluence with the Mississippi, then upriver for the first of many long miles. By now it was November, much too late to think of heading up the Missouri in 1803, even had the Spanish approved. President Jefferson advised Lewis to spend the winter in the St. Louis area. And in no uncertain terms he told his commander to forego a suggested overland wintertime trek across the plains to Santa Fe. Lewis put in at Cape Girardeau, Fort Kaskaskia, and Cahokia. Finally, in early December, he crossed the river to St. Louis, where he would spend most of the next five months.

Meanwhile, William Clark ascended the Mississippi another thirty-five miles or so, and put the Corps of Discovery into winter camp in Illinois (American territory), directly across from the mouth of the Missouri River, on the banks of the River Dubois, or, in English, the Wood River. Clark and his men spent their time drilling, packing, caulking, inventorying supplies, and getting into trouble. Drinking, sleeping, and talking trash are not crimes, unless committed while on military duty. Courts-martial and punishment by lash disciplined the troops.

At Wood River, Clark rebuilt the interior of Lewis's keelboat, transforming a cargo ship into a military vessel. His men constructed lockers on the sides of the hold and the cabin. When the locker tops were up, they served as a shield against attack; when down, they protected the supplies and formed a catwalk for polers. Between the lockers were benches for twenty oarsmen, ten on a side. Mounted on the bow was a bronze swivel cannon, about two feet long, which could fire 18 musket balls at once. Two smaller pirogues were fitted with blunderbusses—short-barreled, wide-bored flintlocks. The Expedition set out as a naval flotilla.

Meriwether Lewis spent most of the winter of 1803–1804 in St. Louis, although occasionally he relieved Clark at Wood River. In the city, Lewis befriended the Choteau brothers, Auguste and his younger sibling Jean Pierre. The Choteaus were prominent river traders who hoped to gain a monopoly over all commerce in Louisiana Territory. They used Lewis, but he used them as well, meeting other powerful figures and learning much about the West. Their close collaboration alienated another important merchant, Manuel Lisa, who would play an equally significant role in the early fur trade of the American West.

The lower Missouri River, all the way up to the Mandan and Hidatsa villages in the middle of North Dakota, was not unknown territory in 1804. British and French traders, traveling overland from Canada, had reached the Mandans as early as 1729. The Verendrye brothers, Louis-Joseph and Francois, had explored the western Dakotas in the early 1740s. James Mackay, a Scottish trader working for Spain, headed upriver to the Mandans in 1787. His compatriot John Evans, another Scotsman looking for a mythical lost tribe of Welsh Indians, wintered there in 1795–1796. There were maps of the lower Missouri; Mackay may have given one to William Clark when he visited the Wood River Camp in January 1804. Lewis obtained others in St. Louis. On their way up the river in 1804, the explorers met numerous French traders, who were married and living with Indian people. Two members of the Expedition, Pierre Cruzatte and François Labiche, had traveled as far as the Platte River. While the Missouri was not exactly a European highway, it had been explored. But now it was in American territory. Lewis and Clark were the first visitors from the United States.

Lewis and Clark were both in St. Louis when the Louisiana Territory officially became American. On March 9, 1804, in an impressive ceremony, the Spanish flag was lowered and the French tricolor raised in its place. (Although France had acquired Louisiana from Spain, the French never occupied or administered the colony. Spanish officials remained in charge. Meriwether Lewis dealt with the Spanish lieutenant governor of Upper Louisiana, Col. Carlos Dehault Delassus.) The next day, March 10, with guns firing and bands playing, the tricolor came down, and the Stars and Stripes flew for the first time west of the Mississippi River. Lewis and Clark would explore American Louisiana in 1804.

Just before departure, Lewis and Clark averted one potential rupture in the Expedition. Both men did themselves proud. When Lewis invited Clark to join him on his western excursion, he assured his friend that "your situation if joined with me in this mission will in all respects be precisely such as my own."[1] Clark applied to the War Department for readmission to the army and for Lewis's rank as captain. But the secretary, Henry Dearborn, citing lack of vacancies, recommended him for a commission as a second lieutenant. That was bad enough, but then the president, Thomas Jefferson, who may have suggested Clark in the first place, forwarded the list to the Senate for confirmation. This was shabby treatment. Could not the president of the United States have lifted a finger to secure a simple promotion?

The rejection arrived in St. Louis, and Lewis regretfully explained the situation to Clark. But the bad news went no further. Lewis told no one else. The men continued to believe that Clark was a captain. Clark even signed documents as "Captain of the Expedition." To this day, the story of the Expedition is one of *Two Captains West,* an Albert and Jane Salisbury name it.[2]

Clark took the rejection like a man, refusing to complain, and never, aside from a confidential explanation years later to his editor, revealing the story. But he was bitter. Upon completion of the Expedition he peremptorily resigned his commission. The incident marks William Clark's magnanimity. A lesser man, in an era when personal slights often resulted in duels, might have quit on the spot and stormed off in a huff. William Clark soldiered on.

Monday, May 14, 1804, was a red-letter day for the Expedition. William Clark and about forty-two men set out from Wood River in the keelboat and two pirogues and proceeded "under a jentle brease" into the mouth of the Missouri River.[3] They were bound for St. Charles, Missouri, a French town about twenty miles away on the banks of the river, where Meriwether Lewis, coming overland from St. Louis, would join them. They were bound, too, for parts unknown—for the High Plains, for the Mandan and Hidatsa Indians, for the Rocky Mountains, the Great River of the West, the Pacific Ocean. Their journey would last longer than anyone expected—for 28 months, 863 days to be exact, 2.36 years. Beyond the Mandans they would see what no white man had ever seen before, and they would describe in detail the wonders and the challenges of the West. Today, we read what they wrote, and experience the same wonders, the same challenges.

The Missouri River, from its headwaters to the Mississippi, is the longest river in North America—longer than the Mississippi by 185 miles (2533 versus 2348 miles). Jefferson's instructions were to explore this river and figure out how to get from it to the Columbia by the most "practicable" route. Lewis and Clark accomplished this task, but it was not easy. The Missouri drains over half a million square miles (second only to the Mississippi) and discharges some 76,300 cubic feet per second (ranking seventh among U.S. rivers, flowing mostly through arid lands). In 1804 this river was unchanneled, undredged, untamed. Flowing at high water because of spring runoffs, the river was fast (4–6 mph), roily, and turbulent. Fallen trees and driftwood created impediments along the banks, which frequently caved in. Sandbars and shifting islands masked the channel. Sawyers (whole trees with their root systems embedded in the river bottom) and sodden logs floating just below the surface threatened to puncture or even capsize the boats. Rowing, poling, towing, and in fair weather sailing the boats was hard work. Somehow the party averaged almost ten miles per day, heading due west across the present state of Missouri.

Lewis and Clark brought along ample supplies of food staples—coffee, salt pork, flour, cornmeal, and an incredible 120 gallons of whiskey—but for the most part the Expedition lived off the fat and the fruit of the land. Hunters headed out every morning to shoot deer, turkeys, wild birds, and even bear. On the lower Missouri the hunters had horses to enable them to range far from the river. Wild fruits and berries supplemented the diet. The river was full of fish—catfish, bass, crappie, and walleye. Private Silas Goodrich, the Expedition's premier angler, could be counted on to put food on the table.

Meriwether Lewis often walked alone along the banks of the Missouri, scouting the countryside, identifying plants and animals, and occasionally hunting. Lewis was the Expedition's premier naturalist. William Clark, a better boatman, stayed on the river, piloting the small flotilla into the West. Incredibly, Clark *surveyed* the entire trek, from Wood River to the Pacific. He used a surveyor's compass to measure angles, from one river bend to another, and then guessed the distance involved. One could, today, working solely from Clark's figures, draw a small-scale map of the entire route of the Expedition across the continent. River channels have changed, however, and huge dams now block the flows of the Missouri, the Snake, and the Columbia Rivers. It is not possible to follow that original route.

Forty-four days out, on June 26, 1804, the Expedition reached the mouth of the Kansas River, on the present Missouri/Kansas border at the site of Kansas City. It had come some four hundred miles, an average of nine per day. The trip across Missouri had not been without tribulations. At a place called The Tavern, a huge cave in sandstone cliffs just two days out of St. Charles, a precipice crumbled under Meriwether Lewis. He tumbled some twenty feet towards the river below. "He Saved himself by the assistance of his Knife," wrote Clark.[4] The next day the keelboat nearly foundered at the Devil's Race Ground, a narrow channel of swift-flowing water. A towrope broke; the vessel almost capsized; spinning around, it careened downstream. Finally a swimmer carried a new rope to shore, and the men tried again—this time successfully. The party encountered eight groups of traders, returning downriver from the near hinterlands. From one such group Lewis and Clark hired Pierre Dorion, a mixed-blood who had lived among the Yankton Sioux, farther upriver. A friendly face might forestall trouble.

Next stop was the mouth of the Platte River, another 200 miles away in a northwesterly direction. The Platte, famous for being a mile wide and an inch deep, was essentially non-navigable, due to rapidly shifting sandbars and channels. Lewis and Clark struggled up the river for a few miles on a sightseeing trip, then gave up and fell back. Little did they know that they were astride the future Oregon Trail, the main route to the West for a later generation.

So far the explorers had not seen an Indian, although they were traveling through country once inhabited, before smallpox thinned their numbers, by Missouris, Otos, Poncas, Pawnees, and Omahas. But they were looking. On July 28 they spotted a Missouri, who lived with a nearby band of Otos and a French trader named Fairfong. The explorers stopped to parley. They named their campsite "Council Bluffs."

President Jefferson's instructions to Lewis emphasized Indian contact. "Treat them in the most friendly & conciliatory manner," he admonished, and learn all you can about them. Lewis took the advice seriously. He and Clark stage-managed Indian conferences with drama and flair. Uniforms, marches, awnings, peace pipes, medals, gifts, and displays of American technology—the air gun, magnifying glasses, compasses, scissors—were all trotted out to impress the natives. Most of the time, it worked.

On the Missouri River, from Council Bluffs to Yankton, South Dakota, the Corps encountered and palavered with three groups of Indians—first, some Otos and Missouris; next, more Otos and Missouris, this time with their head chiefs, Little Thief of the Otos and Big Horse of the Missouris, present; and finally, the Yankton Sioux and their leader, Chief Weuche. The discussions followed a pattern. Soldiers would present arms. Captain Lewis read a long proclamation, emphasizing American sovereignty over the area, preaching peace, and promising beneficial and continuous trade connections. Somehow this speech was translated, either directly (François Labiche spoke Oto), sometimes through several languages, often by sign language (George Drouillard was a master). The chiefs responded. Most of them were more impressed with the trade goods at hand than with loftier ideals of power and peace. Lewis and Clark were not traders—their commercial inventory was for presentation only, and they held on to their guns. Gifts, a little whiskey, and maybe dancing followed.

More than the required discussions marked this eventful stretch of the river. The captains visited the gravesite of the Omaha chief Blackbird, notorious for luring his enemies to dinner and then poisoning them with arsenic. Atop a high hill, the burial spot was decorated with the scalps of Blackbird's victims. (The Omaha, weakened by smallpox, which killed Blackbird himself in 1802, were off hunting buffalo and missed the visit of Lewis and Clark.) One of the privates, Moses Reed, deserted the Expedition, along with a voyageur, La Liberté. Reed was captured, cashiered, and punished by running four gauntlets, to the horror of the attendant Otos. La Liberté got away. George Shannon, the youngest member of the Expedition at 18, got lost while hunting and spent 16 days eating grapes and trying to find the main party. And Sergeant Charles Floyd sickened and died near modern Sioux City, Iowa. He would be the only fatality suffered by the Corps on the entire transcontinental trek. Modern internists believe he died of a ruptured appendix and peritonitis—afflictions fatal anywhere. But there is a strong possibility that he died of arsenic poisoning—Blackbird's last, posthumous victim?

Moving northwesterly through modern South Dakota, the explorers encountered a new environmental landscape—the High Great Plains of the Middle Border. Immense herds of buffalo, deer, and elk assured a hearty, high-protein diet. Strange and different animals appeared—magpies, mule deer, jackrabbits, coyotes, prairie dogs, and pronghorn (the American antelope). The explorers captured a prairie dog by setting up a bucket brigade and flushing the poor critter out of his den with Missouri River water. (The bedraggled animal survived the winter and a trip downriver and ended up in the possession of President Thomas Jefferson.) But nerves were taut. They were approaching Sioux country.

Lewis and Clark must have approached the Teton Sioux villages with much apprehension. All earlier Missouri River travelers had warned of this powerful and aggressive tribe, determined to block free trade on the river. The Sioux, a collection of Brulé, Oglala, and Miniconjou bands, were also riven by internal tensions. Two head chiefs, Black Buffalo and one known as "the Partisan," vied for stature and influence. The Sioux were also expecting a retaliatory raid from the Omaha Indians, to the south. A recent Sioux raid had killed 75 Omaha men, burned 40 lodges, and taken four dozen prisoners. Indeed, the captains could barely communicate with the Sioux. There was no two-way interpreter. Instead, Lewis spoke to Pierre Cruzatte, who knew the Omaha language. Cruzatte translated for an Omaha prisoner, who spoke Sioux. Messages were necessarily garbled and curtailed. This situation was explosive.

It almost blew up. First, Lewis and Clark suspected the Sioux of stealing their last hunting horse. Next, the Indians seemed unimpressed by the Expedition's "demonstration of martial power and Western technology."[5] They wanted more. They wanted the Corps to stop and stay with them, or, at the least, to leave behind a pirogue laden with goods.

No sense supplying your enemies upriver. They wanted whiskey. Lewis and Clark invited the chiefs aboard the keelboat and poured them a few snorts. The Partisan, drunk or acting drunk, jostled Clark. His men grabbed the keelboat's tie-rope. Lewis loaded the swivel gun and the rest of the men stood at arms. Stephen Ambrose describes this confrontation: "It was a dramatic moment. Had Lewis cried 'Fire!' and touched his lighted taper to the fuse of the swivel gun, the whole history of North America might have changed."[6] Finally, Black Buffalo ended the standoff, although not without a heated exchange of threats.

The next day, cooler heads prevailed. The captains and the Sioux sat down to a sumptuous meal at the Indian lodges. Roaring fires, musicians and dancers, songs and stories were intended to impress the newcomers with Sioux hospitality and Sioux power. Women displayed the scalps of vanquished foes. They also offered themselves for the captains' evening enjoyment. Sex symbolically transferred wisdom and power. Lewis and Clark politely declined. The Sioux could not understand their reticence.

One more round of celebration and conflict ensued before the Sioux reluctantly permitted the Expedition to depart. After another ceremonial feast a pirogue struck the keelboat and broke its anchor chain. In the succeeding commotion 200 armed warriors appeared on the river's banks. Lewis and Clark were already on edge because an Omaha prisoner apparently told Cruzatte that the Sioux were determined not to let them leave. But the crisis passed.

The Partisan again acted tough on the morning of departure. Several Sioux held on to the rope and would not let the boats leave. An angry tirade followed. Only the intercession of Black Buffalo, and timely tobacco, eased the situation. Black Buffalo proved the pacifier in these affairs, twice facing down the Partisan and calming the waters.

Lewis and Clark successfully stood up to the bullying Sioux and continued upriver unscathed. But their policies, Jefferson's policies, of intertribal peace and unfettered commerce were in shambles. The Sioux would not lay down their war clubs and take up peaceful trade. They remained as problematic as ever. William Clark did not like them very much. They were "the vilest miscreants of the savage race," and "the pirates of the Missouri."[7] For the Teton Sioux, these were compliments.

By contrast, the Expedition's meetings with the Arikara Indians, who lived in three villages near the mouth of the Grand River (modern

Mobridge, South Dakota), were cordial and amicable. It helped that
Arikara women freely offered sexual favors to the men, and especially
to York, Clark's slave. The Arikara population had been severely
depleted by smallpox. In 1804 they clung to a precarious existence as
suppliers of food and horses to the Sioux, and as middlemen in the
Mandan trade. They promised to abide by American wishes of peace
and commerce. But the Arikara were badly divided politically, and
Lewis and Clark made the naive mistake of elevating one sachem,
Kakawissassa, above the other two. Apparently the Arikara had no
intention of keeping their promises. Within a year or two they too
would become "pirates of the Missouri."

On October 26, 1804, the Corps of Discovery pulled up at the first
of five Indian villages near the mouth of the Knife River, at the great
western bend of the Missouri. There it would spend the next 163 days,
wintering among the friendly Mandan and the not-so-friendly Hidatsa
Indians. This is by far the longest time the Expedition lingered at any
single site on the trip to the Pacific. The men built a triangle-shaped
palisade on the east bank, across the river and about two miles away
from the first Indian village. They named it Fort Mandan and were glad
to have it when winter temperatures reached 40° below and falling.

The Mandans and Hidatsas, two different peoples living peacefully
in the same vicinity, were agricultural tribes, although the Mandans
rode onto the plains to hunt buffalo and the Hidatsa raided all the way
to the Rockies. The Mandans called the inhabitants of the upper two
Hidatsa towns, on the Knife River, the Minitaris ("Minnetaree," for
Lewis and Clark). French-Canadians called them Gros Ventres, or Big
Bellies. A total of some 4,400 people inhabited an area maybe 2 × 8
miles in dimension. This was probably the largest Indian population
anywhere in the Plains or Rockies and larger than the cities of Washington, D.C., and St. Louis at the time. Which are the real "villages"?

The Mandan/Hidatsa villages already constituted a major international trade center or entrepôt, "the central market place of the Northern Plains."[8] Visiting Assiniboine and Cree traders from the northeast
brought items of European manufacture, including guns and ammunition. Cheyenne and Crow Indians from the west arrived with horses
and leather. The Mandans and Hidatsa supplied beans, corn, squash,
and seeds. Although the height of the commercial season had passed,
50 to 70 lodges of Assiniboines showed up in November to trade. Lewis

and Clark, with their keelboat full of American goods, added to this commercial frenzy.

Already, representatives of the great British and French trading companies were on assignment in the area. Most of them worked for the Montreal-based North West Company, including René Jusseaume, whom the Captains mistrusted but employed as an interpreter; François-Antoine Larocque, who wanted to go west with Lewis and Clark; Charles McKenzie, whom Lewis accused of spreading British sedition; Hugh McCracken, High Heney, and maybe others. A couple were employed by the Hudson's Bay Company. Most famous is Toussaint Charbonneau, a Frenchman living with his two Shoshoni wives (one named Sacagawea), who moved his family into Fort Mandan almost immediately.

At their first council with the Indian chiefs, on October 29, Lewis and Clark laid down their diplomatic and economic goals. They sought an alliance among the Mandan, Hidatsa, and Arikara tribes against, first, the Assiniboine and Cree, and second, the Sioux. Part of this plan was military, and part was commercial. The Captains sought to break the power of the Sioux, the pirates of the Missouri, and to wean the Earth Lodge People away from their North West Company connection. Then St. Louis traders would have free run of the river and a monopoly on Mandan-area trade. These new arrangements came with promises of protection from the United States of America.

The Indians were suspicious of this master plan. Although the Mandans told the captains what they wanted to hear, they did not trust the Arikara at all. The Hidatsa were even more reluctant. They disliked the location of Fort Mandan, down among the Mandans. (Lewis and Clark would have been better served to have found a more central location.) They appreciated the benefits of current British and French trade relations. Throughout the winter, they remained more or less aloof from the American party. But Lewis and Clark had done their duty, and they professed their satisfaction.

More mundane matters occupied most of the time. There were constant visitations, especially with Chief Sheheke of the nearby Mandans, and exchanges of food, gifts, and supplies. John Shields, the Expedition's blacksmith, set up a forge and repaired Mandan guns and tools. He even made war axes out of an old corn grinder. Some of these axes showed up among the Nez Perce Indians west of the Continental

Divide less than a year later. Each side marveled at the others' cere-
monies—the Indians at Christmas and New Year's, the explorers at the
"adoption dance" welcoming visitors and the buffalo-calling rite, featuring symbolic sexual exchanges.

Other incidents were more threatening. When a Sioux and Arikara
war party attacked five Mandan hunters, killing one, wounding two,
and stealing nine horses, William Clark assembled twenty-one of his
men to march overland and seek revenge. Chief Big Man was puzzled:
in winter? He figured that the Mandan could deal with the Arikara
upstarts in the spring. Clark and his men, equally puzzled at the Mandan attitude, backed off. Another Sioux raid in February surprised
George Drouillard and a small party hunting about twenty-five miles
from Fort Mandan. The Indians made off with horses and food. This
time Meriwether Lewis led a party including 20 Americans in retalia-
tion. They found no Sioux but compensated by bringing home 2,400
pounds of meat.

The incidents reveal the captains' inability to promote peace on
the plains merely by preaching it. They blamed the Sioux, since these
"vile miscreants" were merely acting the part assigned to them. The
Mandans were more blasé. Incidents like these were normal wintertime
activities. They blamed the Arikara, "*liers* and bad men."[9]

The captains also spent the winter fulfilling Jefferson's instructions to learn all they could about their Native American hosts. They
learned a lot. The observations of Lewis, Clark, and Sergeant John Ordway provide insights and knowledge about Indian politics and military
power, objects of material culture, and tribal practices and beliefs. They
gathered this information in a "Report from Fort Mandan," some
45,000 words in length. Clark's "Estimate of Eastern Indians" (from the
Mississippi to the Rockies) was a massive statistical compilation cover-
ing some fifty tribes. Much of this information appeared on a large map
he prepared. Lewis collected elaborate Indian vocabularies, unfortunately lost, as are many of the original languages. Lewis also learned a
good deal about the geography of the western country ahead.

The information Lewis and Clark amassed about the territory they
were set to explore is amazing. As early as 1796 Jean Baptiste Truteau,
in a report known to the Captains, maintained that the Missouri River
originated in "great mountains of rock," beyond which another "wide
and deep river" flowed "in the direction of the winter sunset" to "a large

body of water, the other bank of which was not visible."[10] Mentally, Europeans had already crossed the continent to the Pacific. Pierre Menard, known as "Old Menard," was an illiterate Frenchman who had lived with the Mandans for twenty years. He died early in 1804, the year of Lewis and Clark. Menard had traveled up the Yellowstone River to visit the Crow nation. He told Truteau about the Chioutounes, or Snake Indians, who lived beyond the Yellowstone.[11] Truteau's companion John Evans learned in 1796 that the Missouri ran *north* between chains of the Rockies before it fell over the eastern chain onto the plains. Evans's map of 1797 depicts "the fall" at the easternmost chain about 500 miles from the Mandan villages.[12] All this information is accurate. Lewis and Clark knew it all even before they left St. Louis.

On January 16, 1805, the Hidatsa chief Le Borgne, "One Eye," visited Lewis at Fort Mandan. He drew "a chart in his way" to display the West.[13] From all their sources, Lewis and Clark gained a remarkably accurate picture of both the geography and the inhabitants of the West. They knew the course of the Missouri River, its headwaters, and its tributaries. They even had some indication of west-slope streams. They had every Northern Plains Indian tribe properly if generally located. Foremost among these was the Shoshoni.

Precisely when the pivotal location and importance of the Shoshoni or Snake Indians came into focus is not entirely clear in the *Journals*. William Clark first identified them almost nonchalantly as "the Snake Indians who inhabit the rockey mountains."[14] A few days later Clark recorded that "a french man by Name Chabonah, who Speaks the Big Belley language visit us, he wished to hire & informed us his 2 Squars were Snake Indians, we engau him to go on with us and take one of his wives to interpet the Snake language."[15] Sometime during their first week among the Mandans, if not earlier, the explorers came to realize that they needed these faraway Native Americans. The Shoshoni would be the last tribe they would encounter on the plains and the first in the mountains. They would need directions, guides, assistance, and horses. They would need an interpreter. They would need Sacagawea.

So the "two Squars of the Rock Mountain" were already essential to the success of the Expedition and the safety of the Shoshoni in wars against the Crow and Hidatsa, a major concern of the Captains. It is hard not to read more into such cryptic lines as "one of the Squars of

Shabownes Squars being Sick," or to sweat out Sacagawea's "tedious" and "violent" labor pains. And who was more important, Sacagawea or Toussaint Charbonneau? Just two weeks before departure, Charbonneau threatened to quit. He wanted to go, but not to work. Lewis and Clark let him twist in the wind for a few days and he came crawling penitently back.[16] What would have happened had he made good on this threat? Would Lewis and Clark have bought his wife? Being Shoshoni, a Snake speaker, was critical. The two Snake girls (one stayed; Sacagawea went) were already integral to the passage.

Once, the Shoshoni Indians were a wide-ranging plains people— all the way from Canada to Mexico. Some time in the eighteenth century they acquired horses and quickly established military supremacy as far north as the Bow and Oldman Rivers. But the benefits of contact were mixed, for smallpox struck the tribe soon afterwards, and when their inveterate enemies, the Blackfeet or Piegans, acquired guns from Cree and Assiniboine traders, the Shoshoni were pushed back into the Rocky Mountains. At the time of Lewis and Clark their main encampment was west of the Continental Divide, on the Lemhi River in modern Idaho. From there the Shoshoni, often in concert with Flatheads and Nez Perces, ventured east into buffalo country on seasonal hunts. There they risked attack by Blackfeet or by marauding bands of Minitaris. On one of these Hidatsa raids, near Three Forks around 1799, young Sacagawea was kidnapped.

How much Lewis and Clark knew about this rapidly changing tribal demography is unclear. Meriwether Lewis placed the Snake Indian villages "on the three forks of the Missouri" in 1805. William Clark believed the Shoshonis "rove on both Sides from the falls about 2500 miles up near the Rock mountain to the head."[17] In other words, the Shoshoni might be anywhere—but it would be best to look for them at the Great Falls of the Missouri. The Great Falls, therefore, became the Expedition's next major destination point.

As the long, cold winter waned, Lewis and Clark began preparing for the next leg of their journey. They sent men upriver to cut and carve six big cottonwood dugout canoes. They readied the keelboat, too heavy for shallow upstream waters, for its return to St. Louis, packed with specimens and collections. Corporal Richard Warfington took along French voyageurs, plus the deserter, Moses Reed, and the mutineer, John Newman. Lewis, Clark, and their party of 31, plus Lewis's dog Seaman, headed the other way.

Notes

1. Lewis to Clark, 19 June 1803, *Letters of the Lewis and Clark Expedition, with Related Documents, 1783–1854,* ed. Donald Jackson, 2 vols. (Urbana: University of Illinois Press, 1978), I, 57–60.

2. Albert Salisbury and Jane Salisbury, *Two Captains West: An Historical Tour of the Lewis and Clark Trail* (Seattle: Superior Publishing, 1950).

3. All quotations are taken from Gary E. Moulton, ed., *The Journals of the Lewis & Clark Expedition,* 13 vols. (Lincoln: University of Nebraska Press, 1983–2001). This quotation is from II, 227, May 14, 1804 (Clark). Hereafter, *Journals.*

4. *Journals,* II, 248, May 23, 1804 (Clark).

5. Indian relations are best described in James P. Ronda, *Lewis and Clark among the Indians* (Lincoln: University of Nebraska Press, 1984), quotation at 32.

6. Stephen E. Ambrose, *Undaunted Courage: Meriwether Lewis, Thomas Jefferson, and the Opening of the American West* (New York: Simon & Schuster, 1996), 170.

7. *Journals,* III, 418, undated (Clark).

8. Quoted in Ronda, *Lewis and Clark,* 75.

9. *Journals,* III, 245, November 30, 1804 (Clark).

10. "Trudeau's [Truteau's] Description of the Upper Missouri," in A. P. Nasatir, ed., *Before Lewis and Clark: Documents Illustrating the History of the Missouri, 1785–1804,* 2 vols. (Lincoln: University of Nebraska Press, 1990), II, 377–81. See also John L. Allen, "Geographical Knowledge and American Images of the Louisiana Territory," *Western Historical Quarterly* 2 (April 1971): 151–70.

11. Bob Saindon, "Old Menard," *We Proceeded On* 13, 2 (May 1987): 4–10.

12. "Captain McKay's Journal," in Nasatir, ed., *Before Lewis and Clark,* II, 498.

13. *Journals,* III, 276, January 16, 1805 (Clark). See also James P. Ronda, "'A Chart in His way': Indian Cartography and the Lewis and Clark Expedition," *Great Plains Quarterly* 4, 1 (Winter 1984): 43–53.

14. *Journals,* III, 210, October 29, 1804 (Clark).

15. *Journals,* III, 228, November 4, 1804 (Clark).

16. *Journals,* III, 232, November 11, 1804 (Clark); 277, January 20, 1805 (Clark); 291, February 11, 1805 (Lewis); 313, March 12, 1805 (Clark).

17. *Journals,* III, 369, undated (Lewis); 436, undated (Clark).

CHAPTER 3

ACROSS THE PLAINS AND OVER THE ROCKIES

The Lewis and Clark Expedition set out from Fort Mandan for the Pacific Ocean on April 7, 1805. "We were now about to penetrate a country at least two thousand miles in width," wrote Lewis, "on which the foot of civillized man had never trodden."[1] The Expedition now consisted of 33 individuals and a dog, traveling upriver in two pirogues and six dugout cottonwood canoes. It was a military expedition, organized and governed by the Rules and Articles of War. Captain Lewis and Lieutenant Clark commanded a party divided into three squads headed by regular army sergeants—John Ordway, Nathaniel Pryor, and Patrick Gass. The sergeants organized evening messes and morning departures and occasionally commanded smaller detachments. They also kept journals—those by Ordway and Gass have survived. Twenty-three privates did the heavy hauling.

An incongruous and decidedly nonmilitary lot filled out the roster. George Drouillard had already proven himself the Expedition's best hunter and a master of Indian sign language. Clark's slave York, the "black white man," cooked for the captains, hunted, and generally made himself useful. Toussaint Charbonneau tagged along and periodically prepared his dinner specialty, "white pudding," or sautéed buffalo sausage. His wife Sacagawea carried her two-and-a-half-month-old son, Jean Baptiste, whom Clark affectionately dubbed "Pomp." Incredibly, this group of hardened, tempered, disciplined, obedient soldiers would complete a grueling 18-month round-trip to the Pacific accompanied by a teenage girl and her baby.

Leaving winter quarters, the route curved around the Great Bend of the Missouri and headed due west to the Rockies. The going was tough—swift spring currents, high winds, blowing sand—but the pace was astonishing—93 miles to the mouth of the Little Missouri in four days. Apprehensive about Assiniboine attack, the party saw no Indians but plenty of game. On April 15, eight days out, it passed the farthest-known point reached by white men—Baptiste Lepage had been there. Ten days later Meriwether Lewis, hiking overland, reached the Yellow-stone River, "the second fabled and mysterious, uncharted river" along the route (after the Platte).[2]

Three days at the confluence was almost relaxing for the members of the Expedition, who celebrated with a gill (4 ounces) of concentrated brandy. But the river called. Entering modern Montana, the Expedition's journalists remarked on the rolling, treeless, Great Plains grasslands; the weather; the river; and always the profusion of game. The high country on either side of the river was "one vast plain, intirely destitute of timber," "level as a bowling green," extending "back as far as the eye can reach." Across these plains swept violent winds, stirring up waves, blowing dust and sand, and bringing at times the rain, snow, ice, and fog of springtime. On the plains lived one of the greatest concentrations of wildlife anywhere in the world. Animals hidden in the mountain fastness today lived in the open before the coming of the white man and his cattle. "We can scarcely cast our eyes in any direction," wrote Lewis, "without percieving deer Elk Buffaloe or Antelopes."[3] Grizzly bears, bighorn sheep, wolves, coyotes, beaver and porcupines abounded, as did geese, ducks, eagles and swan. The Corps lived high on the fat of the land.

Westward the terrain changed. The Missouri Breaks were "truly a desert barren country," the "Deserts of America" for William Clark, "as I do not Conceive any part can ever be Settled, as it is deficent in water, Timber & too Steep to be tilled."[4] Much of that territory now lies submerged under the waters of the Fort Peck Reservoir. Much of it remains unchanged along the wild and scenic Missouri, especially the White Cliffs of the new Missouri Breaks National Monument. "A most romantic appearance," rhapsodized Lewis, as his imagination perceived "a thousand grotesque figures," "the remains or ruins of eligant buildings," and other "seens of visionary inchantment." Lewis also waxed poetic on first seeing the Rocky Mountains, feeling "a secret pleasure in finding myself so near the head of the heretofore conceived boundless Missouri."[5] But he was looking at outliers—the true Rockies were still far away.

Each day brought new adventures. On May 29 a rampaging buffalo stormed through camp at night, damaging weapons and narrowly missing several sleeping men. That day the Corps passed the Judith River and examined what Lewis described as a buffalo jump, where "the remains of a vast many mangled carcases . . . created a most horrid stench."[6] A dram of "sperituous liquors" calmed everyone down. Actually the site was not a *pishkun,* where Indians drove herds over cliffs, but a float collection of animals drowned in the river and swept over the falls.

Earlier, on May 14, the same day that six men took eight shots to bring down a charging grizzly, the white pirogue had capsized. Manned by Charbonneau, who "cannot swim and is perhaps the most timid waterman in the world," the vessel tipped over when a squall of wind caught its square sail, and before the interpreter had recovered his senses, it filled with water. Cruzatte threatened to shoot him if he didn't stop crying to God and grab the rudder. Lewis almost jumped into the raging river 300 yards away before he realized that "I should have paid the forfit of my life for the madness of my project." Aboard the pirogue were the Expedition's papers, instruments, books, medicine, and merchandise. Not all was lost. Sacagawea alertly plucked some papers out of the river. But because, about a week later, duplicate scientific entries appeared in the journals, it is possible that Lewis lost his entire journal of the 1804 trip up the Missouri to Fort Mandan. Small wonder that the unnerved captain "thought it a proper occasion to console ourselves and cheer the sperits of our men and accordingly took a drink of grog and gave each man a gill of sperits."[7]

Thomas Jefferson told Lewis to learn all he could about the southern tributaries of the Missouri. The president believed they originated in a mythical "height of land" and provided access to other river systems, including the Rio Grande and Spanish America. "The Northern waters," he admonished, "are less to be enquired after." Lewis reversed the admonition. Throughout the northern plains he was particularly attentive to the Missouri's northern affluents. The Poplar River might "afford a very favorable communication to the Athebaskay country, from whence the British N. W. Company derive so large a portion of their valuable furs."

The Milk River "might furnish a practicable and advantageous communication with the Saskashiwan river."[8] Clearly Lewis, acting on his own volition or on secret instructions from Jefferson, was deeply concerned with the geopolitical and economic effects of his discoveries. If these rivers came from the faraway north, they might extend the boundary of the United States beyond 49 or 50 degrees and impinge on lucrative British fur-trapping grounds in present Canada.

The Poplar and Milk Rivers produced only speculations. The Marias River demanded action. The Marias posed the central geographical question of the entire Expedition. Swollen by spring runoffs, roily and turbid like the Missouri, the Marias was an unexpected challenge. First of all, it should not have been there. No Indian information prepared the captains for it, and the one northern tributary they had heard of, "the river that scoalds at all others," they took to be the Milk. Why, since Hidatsa maps were otherwise accurate, was the Marias a void? We can only speculate. So little water flows in it for most of the year that maybe Indian informants thought it not worth mentioning. Or perhaps, accustomed to taking an overland shortcut across the base of this north-pointing spike of the Missouri, they had not even known about it. But Lewis and Clark struck the Marias at the height of its spring runoff in a climatic cycle much wetter than now. Moreover, the Marias is the river that dumps the mud into the Missouri. The Missouri, the "Big Muddy," flows clear at the Falls; the Marias, a plains river, first gives the Missouri its chief characteristic.

Which of these rivers was the true Missouri? Which one should the Corps of Discovery navigate? On this question hung the fate of the Lewis and Clark Expedition. As Lewis put it:

> To mistake the stream at this period of the season, two months of the traveling season having now elapsed, and to ascend such stream to the rocky Mountain or perhaps much further before we could inform ourselves whether it did approach the Columbia or not, and then be obliged to return and take the other stream would not only loose us the whole of this season but would probably so dishearten the party that it might defeat the expedition altogether.[9]

To a man, the other members of the party, experienced watermen among them, thought the Marias pointed in their direction. Lewis and Clark were not so sure.

The captains were not about to proceed on hunches. This decision demanded scientific exactitude. Accordingly, Lewis and Clark sent search parties up both rivers; when these proved inconsequential, they set out themselves. Clark went 45 miles up the Missouri, found that it ran swift and true from the west of south, and returned persuaded. Lewis hiked over 60 miles up the Marias, found that it "had it's direction too much to the North for our rout to the Pacific," and made his way back.[10] The mountain ranges they could see from the vicinity—the Highwoods, Big and Little Belts, even the distant front range of the Rockies—supported their assumptions. The biggest problems involved the Arrowsmith map, which Lewis peremptorily revised, and Pierre Cruzatte, an experienced waterman who instinctively favored the Marias. But, sure of their calculations, they made the correct decision and chose the true Missouri. It was a triumph of scientific deduction over seat-of-the-pants reckoning.

Here is an interesting might-have-been. What if the explorers had made the wrong decision at the Marias? Lewis was surely right—the purpose of the Expedition would have been thwarted. But Lewis and Clark were too good as geographers not to have discovered Marias Pass—the lowest pass over the Continental Divide anywhere in the northern Rockies, not found (by John F. Stevens, a railroad engineer) until 1888. Crossing the pass, and following the Middle Fork of the Flathead River, would have brought the party to Flathead Lake, the largest natural freshwater body west of the Great Lakes. From there? Well, they would have been in the Columbia River drainage, but without Indian directions, it was still a long, circuitous way from the Pacific.

The Marias River also halted abruptly the Expedition's astonishing rate of speed since leaving Fort Mandan and interrupted its carefully crafted timetable for reaching the Pacific. In 54 traveling days since April 7 it had covered 884 miles, an incredible average, going upriver during spring runoff, of more than 16 miles per day. Had it maintained this schedule it would have reached the Pacific by early September—time enough, Lewis calculated, to return as far as the head of the Missouri, or perhaps to Fort Mandan before winter. Instead, when early September arrived, the Corps of Discovery found itself in the snow and cold of the Bitterroot Mountains, far from the coast and uncertain of its future.

There were two more Marias particulars. First, during the week the Expedition camped at the river's mouth, Sacagawea almost died. Her loss would have left the Expedition geographically adrift. Sacagawea was "our only dependence for a friendly negociation with the Snake Indians on whom we depend for horses to assist us in our portage from the Missouri to the columbia River."[11] Second, the Marias River came in from the *north*. As far as Lewis explored it in 1805, it was a south-flowing stream. Perhaps the Marias deserved further exploration.

Did a small cloud of doubt cross Meriwether Lewis's mind as he left the Marias confluence on June 11? Had he and Clark made the right decision? One landmark would clinch the argument—the Great Falls of the Missouri. To assure the doubting troopers that they were indeed on the proper river, and to arrive quickly at a final resolution, Lewis decided to march overland. After caching some excess articles and hiding the red pirogue, he set out on the north bank of the Missouri. He paused to admire the august if formidable spectacle of the Rocky Mountains, passed through "a most beatifull and level plain" with "infinitely more buffaloe than I had ever before witnessed," and in two days arrived at the "sublimely grand specticle" of the Great Falls.

Once again, Lewis's poetic nature emerged. For two hours he sat on a rock overlooking "the grandest sight I ever beheld," and at great length he described "the beauty of this majestically grand senery." He could not do justice to "this truly magnificent and sublimely grand object, which has from the commencement of time been concealed from the view of civilized man."[12] No small part of his rapture derived from the certain knowledge that his decision at the Marias had been right.

Proudly, Lewis sent a message to Clark "from the Great falls of the Missouri." The next day he hiked upriver, marveling in turn at each successive cascade. For the Missouri pours onto the plains not over a single cataract but over five separate falls, with intervening rapids. When William Clark surveyed a portage route around these waterfalls, on the south bank of the river, it ran to 18.5 miles across extremely uneven terrain and climbed 400 feet. Clark anticipated "the most perilous and dificult part of our Voyage." Perilous and difficult it was. Indeed, the splendor of the Falls bore an inverse relationship to the hardships of their passage.

Lewis and Clark established a base camp, "lower portage camp," below the falls. There they hid the white pirogue and cached surplus equipment. The six dugouts and other baggage they hauled up "Portage

Creek" (now Belt Creek) to a point affording an easy egress. They built makeshift wheels and axles from cottonwood trees. Then the fun began. Under a broiling sun, plagued by ubiquitous prickly pears whose thorns penetrated even double-soled moccasins, stepping on "sharp points of earth as hard as frozen ground," battered and bloodied by three-inch hailstones, and tormented by mosquitoes, the men, "cooks & all," pushed, hauled, lifted, and carried the boats and baggage across the plains to "upper portage camp" at the White Bear Islands. Constant pulling and shoving over ruts and ravines completely wore out the men; they collapsed and fell asleep at every rest stop. "Their fatiegues are incredible," reported Clark. "Some are limping from the soreness of their feet, others faint and unable to stand for a few minutes." Wind provided the only respite; the men unfurled the sails on the canoes and it blew the trucks along; "this is Saleing on Dry land in every Sence of the word,"[13] Clark commented. Somehow, after a 12-day travail, the portage was over.

Matters now awaited the launching of Meriwether Lewis's vaunted iron boat, an experiment in navigation in the best tradition of the Enlightenment. The contraption was the mountain substitute for the two large and heavy pirogues, already cached. Lewis had carried the metal frame, which weighted 90 pounds, all the way from Harpers Ferry. Outfitted with wooden struts and seats, and covered with 28 elk and 3 buffalo skins, the completed boat was 36 feet long, 4 1/2 feet wide in the beam, and 26 inches deep. It took five men to lift it, and it could bear a cargo of 8,000 pounds. (The iron framework for a boat of that size and carrying capacity must have weighed closer to 200 pounds. Presumably it is still buried beside the Missouri River somewhere in the Great Falls area.)

When Lewis first set his boat upon the water, she floated "like a perfect cork." But problems quickly developed. The stitch holes at the leather seams were too large and the thread/thongs too small. The boat leaked. Lewis wanted to patch the seams with pine pitch, but none was available, so he substituted a composition of charcoal, beeswax, and buffalo tallow. It didn't work. Soon the makeshift caulk separated from the skins and the boat took on too much water to be serviceable. Lewis was "mortifyed." If he had used only buffalo skins, or singed rather than shaved the elk hides, or had some pine pitch . . . No matter. The iron boat was dismantled, and the framework buried.[14]

Twenty-three miles upriver William Clark found a grove of cottonwood trees, not as big as customary but suitable for the emergency. His men quickly cut down two, shaped and hollowed them, loaded them with the iron boat's putative cargo, and the fleet was once more riverworthy.

The Expedition had arrived at the confluence of the Marias and the Missouri on June 2, 1805. It pulled out of Canoe Camp on July 13. Forty full days in the heart of the traveling season had elapsed without getting anywhere. The rapid advance upriver from Fort Mandan ran into a roadblock. The best-laid travel plans went awry, and the captains were worried. They were rapidly running out of time and space—time to cross the Rockies before winter, and space to find the elusive Shoshoni Indians, with their horses and guides. Their list of troubles was lengthening. To the 40-day delay, the long arduous portage, and the failure of the iron boat, was added another particular. On the 4th of July the captains distributed the last of their distilled spirits. They would have no more liquor until they went home. Perhaps the idea of a gill of brandy, and maybe a fast reel from Cruzatte's fiddle, had sustained the men through a hard day. Well, they still had the fiddle.

Where were the Shoshoni? Lewis and Clark expected to discover them at the Great Falls. They were not there, although Lewis found a recently occupied Indian campsite some ten miles away. Maybe they had been scared away. Clark feared "some accident in advance." Despite being the better boatman, he walked most of the way from the Falls to Three Forks, hoping to encounter the Indians before the guns of the party frightened them off. He was "deturmined to . . . find the Snake Indians if possible." He saw smoke and other recent signs, but no Shoshoni. Prickly pears were in bloom—"one of the beauties as well as the greatest pests of the plains."[15] Poor Clark removed 17 thorns from his feet one night.

Lewis brought the main party upstream, past Fort Mountain (Square Butte, where, if he had checked, he would have found a real *pishkun*), past the Smith and Dearborn Rivers, and into "the gates of the Rocky mountains." His description of these "remarkable clifts" matched his mental outlook—"every object here," he wrote, "wears a dark and gloomy aspect." The going was tough, and Lewis helped his crewmen with navigation, learning "to *push a tolerable good pole* in their fraize." He put his troubles in a humorous light: "Our trio of pests still invade and obstruct us," he complained. "These are the Musquetoes eye knats and prickly pears, equal to any three curses that ever poor Egypt laiboured under except the *Mahometant yoke.*"[16]

Let's face it—Lewis and Clark were lost. There's no other word for it. Here they were pushing up the Missouri from the Falls, alarmed that the river seemed to be flowing from the *east* of south, going in the wrong direction, getting further away from the Pacific, off the plains but not yet into the mountains, east of the Rockies when they had figured to be on the Columbia. Surely, if the Shoshoni had been where they were supposed to be, they would have sent the Expedition on an overland short cut. Or, if the Corps had decided to push upstream, Shoshoni women could have tutored Lewis on the matter of a waterproof seam. This was the "where-the-hell-are-we" phase of the Expedition.

Spirits brightened when Sacagawea recognized the country and assured the party that Three Forks and her people were not far ahead. Finally, on July 27, the river party joined Clark's advance guard at "an essential point in the geography of this western part of the Continent"—the Three Forks of the Missouri River.

Lewis and Clark both reconnoitered the three rivers and named them. Their decision to ascend the Jefferson stemmed from the direction of its flow and from Sacagawea's memories. Her nation had come down the Jefferson and camped at Three Forks five or six years earlier. There it had been attacked by the Hidatsa, and Sacagawea had been kidnapped. Now, after resting three days and dressing skins, the Expedition set out up the rapid, shallow, and circuitous river.

"We begin to feel considerable anxiety with rispect to the Snake Indians," Lewis admitted; "if we do not find them or some other nation who have horses I fear the successful issue of our voyage will be very doubtfull." Accordingly, he began to march ahead, seeking an interview with the "yellow gentlemen" he hoped to find. On the first night out he camped alone, finding "a suitable place to amuse myself in combating the musquetoes."[17] He reached the mouth of the Big Hole (Wisdom) River on August 4 and left a note for Clark. Unfortunately, he placed it on a green willow pole, which an enterprising beaver soon cut down. Clark took the wrong turn and ran into a chapter of accidents.

The boatmen's work in an ordinary day was "fatigueing & laborious in the extreen"; they had to "haul the Canoes over the rapids, which Suckceed each other every two or three hundred yards and between the water rapid oblige to tow & walke on Stones the whole day except when we have poleing men wet all day Sore feet &c. &c."[18] Sergeant Ordway and others began to complain, favoring a quick end to river travel. Then came the wrong turn at the Big Hole. The river was overgrown with willows, campsites were wet, a canoe capsized with valuable articles lost, another filled with water, Private Whitehouse was thrown and nearly crushed by a careening boat, and Shannon, who had gone ahead to hunt, got lost. Not until the next day, after nine miserable mistaken miles, did Drouillard, returning to hunt, overtake the wayward party. Back down the Big Hole came Clark. The mishap cost the party two days' time, and time was precious.

On August 8 Sacagawea recognized Beaverhead Rock, a massive stone outcrop near the river of the same name that bears, from a distance, a striking resemblance to a swimming beaver. The Shoshoni were nearby, just to the west, she said. Desperate, Lewis again forged ahead with three men, Drouillard, Shields, and Hugh McNeal, determined to find the Indians "if it should cause me a trip of one month." The group continued up the Beaverhead and, after one false start, turned west toward the Continental Divide at Horse Prairie Creek. This time Lewis left a note for Clark on a *dry* willow pole.

Marching up a gradual slope on the morning of August 11, with his men as flankers, Lewis spotted a lone Indian horseman. Incredibly, after a 1,200-mile journey from Fort Mandan through territory peopled by Assiniboine, Atsina, Blackfeet, and Crow tribes, this was the first Native American encountered by the Expedition. Lewis tried to draw him in, laying down a blanket, rolling up his sleeve to show white skin, and shouting "*tab-ba-bone*," the Shoshoni word, he thought, for "friend." (The word may have meant the opposite, "enemy." One scholar uses this demonstration to argue that Lewis shaved while out West. Otherwise, a bushy beard would have immediately identified him as European.) Unfortunately, the flankers spooked the horseman; he wheeled and galloped off. Lewis was angry and "abraided" his men.[19]

Not until two days later did Lewis befriend a sizeable Shoshoni contingent. The Snake Indians were not where they were supposed to be—not at the Great Falls, not at the Three Forks, not even in America. They were west of the Continental Divide, on the Lemhi River in modern Idaho. Lewis crossed the Divide on August 12. McNeal straddled the uppermost streamlet and thanked God he had "lived to bestride the mighty & heretofore deemed endless Missouri." Lewis drank deeply from "the most distant fountain" that provided its waters. (Geographers today place the source of the Missouri not at Lemhi Pass on the Bitterroot Range but in the Centennial Mountains to the west of Yellowstone National Park. No matter; the symbolism is appropriate.)

Crossing the Continental Divide is a quintessential moment in the story of the Lewis and Clark Expedition. Imagine this exquisite scene. Here is Meriwether Lewis, hiking resolutely up the east slope of the Bitterroots. What is he thinking? He cannot have had too many illusions remaining about the Rockies, but there must have been the faintest hope, the tiniest possibility, that on the other side of the mountain he would see the great river of the West, flowing toward the setting sun. He had come to the far edge of America, and he was ready for his reward. And what *did* he see? "Immense ranges of high mountains still to the West of us with their tops partially covered with snow." In August! He must have felt as if his stomach had suddenly imploded. Where he had hoped against hope to see his dream come true—Jefferson's dream, Christopher Columbus's dream, the dream of a Northwest Passage—he saw range after range of purple mountains' majesties, receding to the west, receding beyond vision. One thought, and one thought only, must have gripped him like a vise: How are we going to get through that?

Lewis and his men pushed on, across the Divide, across the border into territory claimed by Great Britain, Spain, and even Russia. A military expedition entering foreign country without permission is an act of war, but they faced no opposition. Soon they "tasted the water of the great Columbia river."[20] The next day he used "three female savages" to win, at last, a friendly reception from the long-sought Shoshoni Indians. A band of some sixty warriors, happy he was not an enemy, embraced him so thoroughly he became "heartily tired of the national hug." But Chief Cameahwait conveyed "unwelcome information."[21] The river Lewis thought was the Columbia ran north, then cut west through impassable canyons. How were they to proceed?

Cameahwait was also reluctant to lead his people back to the Beaverhead with Lewis, who needed help transporting his baggage across the Divide. The Shoshoni feared him "in league with the Pahkees," luring them "into an ambuscade where their enimies were waiting." His situation, Lewis perceived, "was not entirely free from danger." Indeed, the ensuing two days constitute the most delicate, touch-and-go period of the entire Expedition, rivaled only by the Teton confrontation. Alternately threatening and cajoling the Shoshoni, Lewis persuaded them, against their better judgment, to accompany him back to Camp Fortunate to await Clark and the boats. When Cameahwait wavered, Lewis challenged his manhood; the Indian boasted that "he was not affraid to die." Approaching the river junction, Lewis's imagination ran wild; he conjured an "unfortunate accedent" wherein "some of there enimies had straggled hither at this unlucky moment." Apprehensive lest the skittish Indians flee, he pledged ultimate faith by handing Cameahwait his gun; "if I deceived him . . . he might shoot me." He deliberately misled the chief by falsifying the note he had left for Clark—"a strategem," he admitted, which "set a little awkward." He "entertained various conjectures myself with rispect to the cause of Capt. Clarks detention." "My mind was in reallity quite as gloomy all this evening as the most affrighted indian," he remembered. For neither the first nor the last time he personalized the Expedition: "I slept but little as might be well expected, my mind dwelling on the state of the expedition which I have ever held in equal estimation with my own existence."[22]

Lewis's sigh of relief the next morning was almost audible, when Clark and the main party finally arrived. There, at the head of the Beaverhead River, the storybook reunion occurred—Sacagawea turned out to be Cameahwait's long-lost sister. The Chief welcomed her somewhat stoically, but Sacagawea wept and wailed at seeing her brother and other relatives. If the Lewis and Clark Expedition were a novel, this meeting would be too fanciful to contemplate. The captains must have congratulated themselves for their foresight in bringing her along from Fort Mandan.

The Shoshoni odyssey was not yet over. Lewis had still to firm up the logistics of transporting baggage across the Divide. He remained at Camp Fortunate for a week, caching equipment, sinking canoes, and trussing up his parcels. When at last he set out once again up Horse Prairie Creek with some one hundred Shoshoni, he was shocked to learn from Charbonneau, who had known about it all day, that Cameahwait and his band intended to desert him in mid-march and decamp east for buffalo country. Lewis was stunned and alarmed lest he be stranded in the Rockies without horses or help. He acted quickly and firmly. First, he upbraided Charbonneau "with some degree of asperity." Next, he tongue-lashed Cameahwait and shamed him into foregoing his buffalo hunt and continuing his assistance.[23]

The close call left Lewis nervous as fits. The pressure of the Shoshoni negotiations possibly explains why he abruptly stopped writing his journals. For two weeks the Expedition, in his mind, had teetered on the brink of failure, and, in a highly symbolic sense, it had failed. The Northwest Passage was mountains, not water. Still, crossing the Continental Divide with Shoshoni help and horses represented a crowning diplomatic triumph for Lewis. It was his finest hour.

Lewis had not entirely believed Cameahwait when the Indian described the difficulties of a waterway to the west. He had to see for himself. Maybe he refused to believe his visual senses on top of the mountain, or maybe he was just being depressingly thorough. But on August 18 he sent William Clark and eleven axmen ahead, across the pass and down the Lemhi and Salmon Rivers to confirm the bad news. In six days Clark traveled 20 miles down the River of No Return, becoming "perfectly satisfied as to the impracticality of this route either by land or water."[24]

Clark took with him the Shoshoni guide Toby, who, along with the Hidatsa chief who mapped the West for Lewis and Clark, stands as the single Native American most important to the geographical success of the Expedition. Once persuaded of the impossibility of the river route, Clark took charge of the Expedition and put it, it turned out, at considerable risk. William Clark rolled the dice on the Expedition's greatest gamble. On his own, without consulting Lewis, and against the advice of the rest of the Shoshoni Indians, Clark hired Toby to guide the Expedition all the way to the Clearwater River.

Clark's decision was a bold, audacious, uncertain, potentially dangerous move. He entrusted the fate of the entire Expedition to the hands of one old Indian, who was somewhat unsure of the path across the Bitterroots and who, alone among his people, claimed knowledge of the Nez Perce Trail over Lolo Pass. As Lewis later put it: "Thus situated we attempted with success those unknown formidable snow clad Mountains on the bare word of a Savage while 99/100th of his Countrymen assured us that a passage was impracticable."[25] Why did Clark do it?

The Expedition was desperate. At a time when it had expected to be approaching the Pacific Ocean, it was locked in the mountain fastness of the Rockies. It was off course, still lost, uncertain of its options, and unwilling to turn back. When looking for something to grasp, a straw is better than nothing. Clark grasped.

With Clark's decision went the certain knowledge that the geography of the American West needed serious reevaluation. The Rockies were not the Blue Ridge Mountains of Virginia. More than a mere half-day's portage was required to move from one river system to another. The Lewis and Clark Expedition was in for a long, often arduous, over-land trek by foot and horse across those "immense mountains still to the west of us."

Moreover, the Rockies represented "the first major change of environment, ecology, and physiography encountered by the expedition west of St. Louis."[26] Lewis and Clark were veteran river travelers, but neither they nor any other American had ever seen anything like the awesome escarpments of the Shining Mountains. This place was clearly a new experience—the most unusual, unique, and challenging environment anywhere on the trail. Journal entries capture the mystique:

> rough high hills . . . deep gullies . . . the stone lay one on another and holes so that the horses could Scarsely git along without break-ing their legs . . . huge rugged hills . . . a Mountain nearly as Steep as the roof of a house . . . rockey hill Sides where our horses were in [perpetual] danger of Slipping to Ther certain distruction & up & Down Steep hills, where Several horses fell, Some turned over, and others Sliped down Steep hill Sides, one horse Crippeled & 2 gave out . . . verry rough and rockey. the mountains make close on each Side of the creek and high covred with pine. this is a verry lonesome place.[27]

"This is a very lonesome place." Although some three dozen explor-ers and Indians constituted the party, it was lonely in the Rockies. That happens when you know not where you are, stranded in a faraway, unknown place. Travelers need a lodestone, a reference point, a familiar setting. For the moment, William Clark was adrift.

It might have helped had Toby known the route. There is a rela-tively easygoing, treeless Indian trail between the North Fork of the Salmon and the East Fork of the Bitterroot River, but Toby did not take it. Instead he struck out over the mountaintops, heading due north on a journey whose precise route still mystifies scholars. Today's U.S. Highway 93, following roughly the same route, crosses Lost Trail Pass—named for Old Toby. "Pilot lost his way," Clark noted ruefully.[28]

Descending from the Bitterroots on September 4, the Expedition encountered its second mountain Indian tribe. Located on the East Fork of the Bitterroot at modern Sula, Montana, Lewis and Clark met "a part of the Tushapau nation," the "Eoote-lash-Schute" Indians, whom Clark was apparently the first to call "Flatheads." Clark counted 33 lodges, about eighty men among a population of 400, and noted especially 500 "ellegant horses."[29] He bought 13. Unfortunately, the Expedition was in a hurry; it spent barely forty-eight hours among the Flatheads, and Clark's journal entries are brief to the point of being cryptic. It is inconceivable that Meriwether Lewis, had he been obeying orders and keeping a record, would have allowed the Flatheads to slip by with so little ink.

Thus there is no follow-up commentary on the startling revelation found only in the journals of Private Joseph Whitehouse and Sergeant John Ordway. From Whitehouse:

> They tell us that we can go in 6 days to where white traders come and that they had Seen bearded men who came [to] a river to the North of us 6 days march but we have 4 mountains to cross before we come on that River.[30]

This important geopolitical information, which probably refers to the employees of David Thompson's North West Company on the upper Kootenai River in southern British Columbia, ought to have been of intense interest to the captains and their superiors. Maybe it was, but on the record there is silence.

From Ross's Hole—the name given to the valley of the East Fork by the British fur trader Alexander Ross in 1822—the Expedition quickly made its way north down the Bitterroot Valley, with its bottomlands described as "pore & stoney." Near the mouth of Lolo Creek the party paused at a campsite named by Lewis "Travellers rest," after a crossroads somewhere in South Carolina. There, on September 9, 1805, Old Toby casually dropped the single most important piece of geographical information found anywhere in the entire corpus of the journals of Lewis and Clark. "Our guide could not inform us," Lewis wrote, where this river [the Bitterroot] discharged itself into the columbia river he informed us that it continues it's course along the mountains to the N. as far as he knew it and that not very distant from where we then were it formed a junction with a stream nearly as large as itself which took it's rise in the mountains near the Missouri to the East of us and passed through an extensive valley generally open prairie which forms an excellent pass to the Missouri. the point of the Missouri where this Indian pass intersects it, is about 30 miles above the *gates of the rocky mountain* . . . the guide informed us that a man might pass to the missouri from hence by that route in four days.[31]

Toby described a shortcut from Travellers Rest to the Missouri River, across the top of the U-shaped route the Expedition had followed. The "stream nearly as large as itself" is Lewis's "Valley plain" river, today's Clark Fork of the Columbia. The "extensive valley generally open prairie" is the Clark Fork and Little Blackfoot Valley, on the road to modern Helena, Montana. Thirty miles above the Gates is just east of Helena, on the Missouri. Four days is a long cry from the 52 days of rugged travel the Expedition had already expended. Right then and there Lewis and Clark decided that if they ever got back this way they would split up and try that route.

But why did the Expedition not descend the Clark Fork, which Lewis rightly figured flowed northwest to the "Tacootchetesse," or Columbia River, and which provides, via Lake Pend Oreille, an all-water route to the Pacific? There are three responses to this puzzle. First, Lewis had learned, however vaguely, that the Clark Fork takes a decidedly roundabout route to the ocean. It flows northwest into Lake Pend Oreille, out of the lake due north (as the Pend Oreille River) into modern Canada, and empties into the Columbia, which describes a huge letter *S* in modern Washington State before straightening out for the Pacific. It would be absolutely impossible to reach the ocean by this route before winter—indeed, before spring. Second, Lewis noted "the circumstance of their being no sammon" in the Bitterrroot River, which indicated "that there must be a considerable fall in it below."[32] If salmon could not come upriver, the Expedition might not be able to go down. (Kettle Falls, on the Columbia River in Washington State, was such an obstacle; it is now inundated by the waters of Franklin D. Roosevelt

Lake behind Grand Coulee Dam.) Finally, Toby recommended a route, more or less directly east to west, over Lolo Pass and the Bitterroot Mountains to the Clearwater, Snake, and Columbia Rivers. It was the shortest and most direct route to the ocean. The Bitterroots were already covered with snow, but Lewis "felt perfectly satisfyed, that if the Indians could pass these mountains with their women and Children, that we could also pass them."[33] Of course, the Indians crossed in the summertime, when they could see the trail.

For seven miles the Lolo Trail followed a good, mostly level, Indian road. Then it hit the hills—"a most intolerable road on the Sides of the Steep Stoney mountains." The party's travails were only beginning. Crossing the Bitterroot Mountains during twelve days in September constituted the most arduous, physically discomforting, and dangerous segment of the entire trip. Early snowfalls hid the trail; Toby could not find it; he led the party into rugged country made worse by heavy timber downfall. There was no game in the mountains; everyone was hungry, and one by one they killed and ate three colts. Horses slipped and rolled down steep hills; Clark's writing desk, lugged all the way west, was smashed up. Eight inches of new snow one day left Clark "wet and as cold in every part as I ever was in my life," and "fearfull my feet would freeze."[34] The Expedition soon left impassable Lochsa river banks for high ridges just to the north. At one point level country lay ahead—40 miles ahead. Trudging from one summit to another wore out both men and horses and put the entire Expedition at risk.

Finally William Clark and six men forged ahead to find food and warmth. First they found a stray horse, which ended up as breakfast. Clark hung the rest of the animal on a tree for Lewis. Then they reached the Weippe Prairie, on the western edge of the wide Rockies, and the home of the Nez Perce Indian tribe. The Nez Perce welcomed this strange group with dried salmon cakes, berries, and camas roots. The sudden change of diet produced intense gastrointestinal distress, which Clark exacerbated with laxatives and emetics. Two days later Lewis and the rest of the party received the same nourishment, with the same results. Everyone was sick; Clark's journal "is practically a hospital daybook."[35] Had the Nez Perce been at all warlike the Lewis and Clark Expedition would have ended right there on the Weippe Prairie in modern Idaho.

Notes

1. *Journals,* IV, 9, April 7, 1805 (Lewis).

2. Quoted in Donald Jackson, "At the Mouth of the Yellowstone: An Introduction," *Among the Sleeping Giants: Occasional Pieces on Lewis and Clark* (Urbana.: University of Illinois Press, 1987), 1–11, at 2.

3. *Journals,* IV, 96, 121, 85, May 1, 7, April 29, 1805 (Lewis).

4. *Journals,* IV, 205–6, May 26, 1805 (Clark).

5. *Journals,* IV, 225–27, 201, May 31, 26, 1805 (Lewis).

6. *Journals,* IV, 215–16, May 29, 1805 (Lewis).

7. *Journals,* IV, 152–53, May 14, 1805 (Lewis).

8. *Journals,* IV, 103, 124, May 3, 8, 1805 (Lewis). The Milk is "the river that scoalds at all others."

9. *Journals,* IV, 246, June 3, 1805 (Lewis). On the Marias dilemma see John L. Allen, "Lewis and Clark on the Upper Missouri: Decision at the Marias," *Montana the Magazine of Western History* 21, 3 (July 1971): 2–17. Aaron Arrowsmith, a British cartographer, had guessed the latitude of the Missouri River incorrectly.

10. *Journals,* IV, 260, June 6, 1805 (Lewis).

11. *Journals,* IV, 299, June 16, 1805 (Lewis).

12. *Journals,* IV, 283–85, June 13, 1805 (Lewis)

13. *Journals,* IV, 295, 328–29, 332–33, June 14, 23, 25, 1805 (Clark).

14. *Journals,* IV, 354–56, 368–69, July 3, 9, 1805 (Lewis).

15. *Journals,* IV, 401, 405, July 18, 19, 1805 (Clark).

16. *Journals,* IV, 402–3, 423, July 19, 24, 1805 (Lewis).

17. *Journals,* IV, 435–37, July 27, 1805 (Lewis); V, 15, July 30, 1805 (Lewis).

18. *Journals,* V, 43, August 4, 1805 (Clark).

19. *Journals,* V, 59, 68–70, 72 n. 1, August 8, 11, 1805 (Lewis).

20. *Journals,* V, 74, August 12, 1805 (Lewis).

21. *Journals,* V, 78–81, August 13, 1805 (Lewis).

22. *Journals,* V, 97, August 15, 1805 (Lewis). The "Pahkees" were the Hidatsa. *Journals,* V, 103–6, August 16, 1805 (Lewis).

23. *Journals,* V, 165–66, August 25, 1805 (Lewis).

24. *Journals,* V, 154–55, August 23, 1805 (Lewis).

25. Lewis to ?, 14 October 1806, *Letters of the Lewis and Clark Expedition with Related Documents, 1783–1854,* ed. Donald Jackson, 2 vols. (Urbana: University of Illinois Press, 1962), I, 339.

26. Harry M. Majors, "Lewis and Clark Enter the Rocky Mountains," *Northwest Discovery* 7, 30–31 (April–May 1986): 94.

27. *Journals,* V, 183, 185–86, September 2, 3, 1805 (Clark); IX, 215–17, August 31–September 3, 1805 (Ordway); XI, 294–98, August 31–September 3, 1805 (Whitehouse).

28. Quoted in Majors, "Lewis and Clark Enter the Rocky Mountains," 101.

29. *Journals,* V, 187–89, September 4–5, 1805 (Clark).

30. *Journals,* IX, 218, September 4, 1805 (Ordway); XI, 299, September 4, 1805 (Whitehouse).

31. *Journals,* V, 192, September 9, 1805 (Lewis).

32. Ibid.

33. *Journals,* V, 90–91, August 14, 1805 (Lewis). Cameahwait had vaguely referred earlier to this Nez Perce trail.

34. *Journals,* V, 201, 209, September 12, 16, 1805 (Clark).

35. Bernard DeVoto, ed., *The Journals of Lewis and Clark* (Boston: Houghton Mifflin, 1953), 241.

CHAPTER 4

THE COLUMBIA AND CLATSOP WINTER

Lewis and Clark had crossed the Rocky Mountains—the most unexpected, circuitous, time-consuming, and potentially perilous segment of the entire journey. There were mountains back east, and rivers, but nothing like these. No American had ever seen anything like these mountains—high, wide, and incredibly rugged. Contrary to understanding, the Rockies were not like the Appalachians, not a single chain of easily passable hills. The Rockies were chain after chain of mountains—more than 50 named outcroppings—and some 250–300 miles wide at these latitudes. Imagine crossing the same north-south range (the Bitterroots) three times on an east-west journey, as Lewis and Clark did! Were they lost?

The miserable, starving, bedraggled troupe that stumbled out of the Bitterroot Mountains onto the Weippe Prairie in September 1805 had completed a stupendous achievement. They had described and defined the American West. The rest of the trip was downhill.

Clark had already met the Nez Perce chieftain Twisted Hair before he and Lewis conducted a formal parley on September 23. Twisted Hair and his people were gracious hosts; their guests promised goods, guns, and prestige. One old Nez Perce woman, Watkuweis, had been treated well by whites in faraway Montreal, where she had been taken as a child. She favored hospitable treatment for Lewis and Clark. Twisted Hair took the party to a grove of ponderosa pine trees on the nearby Clearwater ("Kooskooski") River. There, over the next 12 days, the men built five dugout canoes for the float to the Pacific. They used the Indian method of burning and scraping—much easier, and faster, than pure adze work. Lewis had the party's 38 horses branded with an instrument he'd carried all the way from Harpers Ferry: US Cap^T. M. Lewis. (The brand can still be seen at the Oregon Historical Society in Portland.) The Nez Perce promised to look after the animals over the winter.

On October 7, for the first time since November 14, 1803, on the Ohio River, the Lewis and Clark flotilla was going with the flow. Twisted Hair and his fellow chief Tetoharsky accompanied the party down the Clearwater River. They would introduce the captains to the increasingly numerous peoples on the Snake and Columbia Rivers. Old Toby and his son were along, but soon, their services no longer needed and perhaps worried about their safety in a strange new territory, they absconded without notice, stole two horses from the Nez Perce, and headed home.

The rivers to the Pacific ran swift, with many rapids. Their passage was not without accident. Sergeant Gass's boat hit a rock on the Clearwater, split open, and filled with water, which spoiled and ruined valuable goods. The men mended it with pine pitch. The Snake contained 51 named (later) rapids. In late-season low water they were worse than usual. Sometimes the men portaged; more often, to save time, they ran the rapids.

Clark thought the Snake was actually the Salmon—still "Lewis's River." His geography was intuitive but not accurate—the Salmon is actually a tributary of the Snake, falling into it 50 miles above the mouth of the Clearwater. "Lewis's River" became the South Fork of the Columbia, after the Expedition reached that critical point on October 16.

The party was still eating dried salmon and roots and still suffering severe stomach pains. One new food item appeared—Indian dogs. At the mouth of the Columbia, Clark bought 40 of them, either dead or alive. Clark disliked dog, but "for the first time for three weeks past I had a good dinner of Blue wing Teel," he wrote on October 14. Indians grew more numerous, all of them catching and drying salmon. Fish could be seen "at a deabth of 15 or 20 feet" on the Columbia.[1] Clark paddled 10 miles upriver to the mouth of the Yakima.

Down the Columbia at last! Today the river is a series of wide, still reservoirs, behind the John Day, McNary, Dalles, and Bonneville Dams. (There are 14 dams on the main stem of the Columbia River and more than 500 in the basin.) In 1805 the river ran swiftly by numerous islands, outcroppings, shoals, and huge chunks of basalt from age-old lava flows. On one good day the party made 42 miles, despite a "verry bad rapid" and a "chane of rocks." Then came a 55-mile stretch containing Celilo Falls, and the Short and Long Narrows. Unlike the Great Falls of the Missouri, those of the Columbia were hindrances to pass, not wonders to behold. The men portaged the goods around the right side of Celilo and muscled the canoes around the left. At the Short Narrows, where "the whole of the Current of this great river must at all Stages pass thro' this narrow chanel of 45 yards wide," Clark amazed Indian spectators by running the boats directly into "this agitated gut swelling, boiling & whorling in every direction." Practice makes perfect; the next day the party ran the Long Narrows. Although two of the canoes took on water, Clark was "extreamly gratified and pleased."[2]

All along the Columbia, Indians were drying salmon on scaffolds, then pounding and packing it into grass and rush baskets lined with fish skin. Clark calculated that each basket weighed 90–100 pounds; once he "counted 107 Stacks of dried pounded fish . . . which must have contained 10,000 w. of neet fish."[3] This staple lasted two or three years and was a prime article of commerce. More and more European trade goods showed up in Indian homes. At nearly every stop Clark bought some dogs for dinner.

For nearly a week the Expedition negotiated the Cascades of the Columbia, the Grand Rapids running through the Columbia River Gorge to Beacon Rock, where tidal fluctuations and sea otters bespoke the Pacific. The "Great Shute" compressed the river to a width of "150 paces in which there is great numbers of both large and Small rocks, water passing with great velocity forming & boiling in a most horriable manner." The men portaged the goods and rolled the canoes over logs. They were now out of the mountains, the river was wider, and although Indians were "thievishly inclined," there were fewer of them.[4]

"*Ocian in view!* O! the joy," wrote William Clark on November 7, "this great Pacific Octean which we have been So long anxious to See."[5] The ocean was still more than 20 miles away, but the Corps of Discovery had entered the wide Columbia River estuary. Their joy would have been stillborn had they known what a miserable month was in store for them. Near-permanent bad weather and no level places to camp were the main problems. It would be a month before they found a winter campsite and seven weeks before they moved into winter quarters. And their troubles were only beginning.

Cold, "disagreeable," and "wet as water could make them," the party slowly made its way along the north shore of the estuary, in present-day Washington State. It spent five days camped on a driftwood log floe, fighting "most tremendious waves" and torrents of rain. It spent 10 days at Chinook Point, during which time both Lewis and Clark led separate exploring parties to Cape Disappointment and north along the Pacific coast. Clark met numerous Chinook Indians and traded with them for furs and food. He also met a chief's old wife "with her 6 young Squars" who were looking for action.[6] The weather remained tempestuous, the dried fish was a monotonous diet, and the women were ugly. It was time to move.

Visiting Clatsops from the south shore told of high ground with many elk. Lewis and Clark staged an election. The choices: stay there, move upriver, or cross to Clatsop country. Both Sacagawea and York voted. On November 26 the party returned to Pillar Rock, crossed the Columbia, and camped on Tongue Point, just east of modern Astoria, Oregon. Lewis moved on to find a permanent spot; he selected high ground near the Netul (now Lewis and Clark) River, which flows into Young's Bay. Clark was delighted to leave, since "The Sea which is imedeately in front roars like a repeeted roling thunder and have rored in that way ever Since our arrival in its borders which is now 24 Days Since we arrived in Sight of the Great Western Ocian, I cant say Pasific as Since I have Seen it, it has been the reverse." Before moving, he carved a message: "William Clark December 3rd 1805. By Land from the U. States in 1804 & 1805."[7] The message matched that of Alexander Mackenzie, twelve years earlier, at Bella Coola, in modern British Columbia. The Corps gathered on December 7 and began to build Fort Clatsop.

Winter at Fort Clatsop was the most frustrating, unfulfilling, monotonous segment of the entire Expedition. Lewis and Clark might not even have been there, had they come straight west instead of taking their circuitous Rocky Mountain detour. No ships greeted them in the Columbia River estuary; they arrived after the 1805 sailing season ended and left before the 1806 season began. The men built a small, enclosed set of cabins, a "fort," just 50 feet by 50 feet (2,500 square feet), barely 50 percent of which was living space. In these cramped quarters 33 people spent 89 days and nights, mostly keeping dry. Watching each other cut and sew 358 pair of elk-skin moccasins is not an antidote to ennui. Cooped up and crowded, cabin fever surely ensued. "Nothing worthy of notice occurred today" is the most repetitious refrain in the journals of Lewis and Clark.

All the exciting events happened early. Seeing the ocean—the reward at the end of a long and arduous journey—inspired wonder and awe. Christmas 1805 coincided with the move into the fort. A salt-making contingent took five large kettles to the beach at modern Seaside, Oregon, and a rotating crew of three spent eight weeks boiling ocean water to produce three bushels of this precious commodity. News of a beached whale on Cannon Beach, just south of Tillamook Head, inspired Clark and a large party, including Sacagawea, who insisted upon the trip, to inspect the site. Clark hoped to obtain some blubber and oil, for cooking flavors. But the local Tillamook Indians had already stripped the animal. They reluctantly parted with 300 pounds of blubber and a few gallons of oil.

Winter at Fort Clatsop was one long litany of complaint. At the top of the list was the weather. It rained on all but 6 of the 137 days the Corps of Discovery spent at the mouth of the Columbia. Constant rain was gloomy and depressing. "O! How horriable is the day," complained William Clark one day. "O! How disagreeable is our Situation dureing this dreadfull weather." "The rain Continues," he added, "with Tremendious gusts of wind, which is Tremds." Once, while camping, Clark reported, "The winds violent Trees falling in every derection, whorl winds, with gusts of rain Hail & Thunder . . . Certainly one of the worst days that ever was!"[8]

Neither Lewis nor Clark liked the Columbia River Native Americans very much. They looked strange. "Those Indians are low and ill Shaped all flat heads," noted Clark. "[T]hey are badly clad & illy made, Small." "The Men are low homely and badly made, Small Crooked legs large feet and . . . flattened heads." The women were worse. "I think the most disgusting sight I have ever beheld is these dirty naked wenches."[9]

Coastal Indians were also crooks, by the lights of Lewis and Clark. They stole everything not nailed down—an ax, a spoon, a tomahawk, and rifles. Lewis wrote of "their great averice and hope of plunder." Indians also drove hard bargains in trade and commerce; their capabilities as capitalists irritated Lewis and Clark. "[T]hey are tite Deelers," complained Clark, "Close deelers, & Stickle for a verry little, never close a bargain except they think they have the advantage." "Those people ask double & tribble the value of everry thing they have to Sell." "[T]hey are great higlers in trade," concurred Lewis, "and if they conceive you anxious to purchase will be a whole day bargaining for a handful of roots." "I therefore believe," he generalized, "this trait in their character proceeds from an avaricious all grasping disposition."[10]

Next to the weather, the biggest daily downer at Fort Clatsop was the diet. The menu was monotonous—"pore" or spoiled elk meat, or maybe "Some Spoiled pounded fish and a fiew roots." The Expedition wintered where it did because elk lived there, but hunting trips ranged farther and farther afield; killed meat did not freeze and rotted before consumption. "We are now liveing on Spoiled Elk which is extreamely disagreeable to the Smel. as well as the taste," wrote Clark. "We have nothing to eate but Pore Elk meet, nearly spoiled; & this accident of Spoiled meet, is owing to wormth & the repeeted rains, which cause the meet to tante before we Can get it from the woods."[11] Occasionally, dried berries, dogs, and candlefish provided a welcome respite.

It is difficult to sympathize with Lewis and Clark over their constant whining about food. Here they are on the Columbia River estuary, one of the most fertile fisheries anywhere in the world, and they eat "pore elk." They are four miles from the Pacific Ocean. Lewis wrote about, but apparently did not eat, "the Clam, perriwinkle, Common muscle, cockle, and a Species [of shellfish] with a circular flat Shell." In nearby waters were skate, flounder, salmon, sturgeon, char, and trout. What a bouillabaisse! And "verry large water fowls" graced the neighborhood—swan, geese, crane, ducks, plover, and brants.[12] "Pore elk" was not the only menu item.

Imagine spending 137 nights in a flea-ridden bedroll. Even before moving into Fort Clatsop the explorers "found great numbers of flees which we treated with the greatest caution and distance." "I was attacked most violently by the flees," reported Clark, " and they kept up a close Siege dureing the night." "We can't get them out of our robes & Skins." "We have regularly to kill them out of our blankets." Fleas moved right into the fort with the men. Lewis despaired. "We shall not devest ourselves of this intolerably troublesome vermin during our residence here," he lamented.[13]

Incessant rain, crowded quarters, and poor nutrition added up to a rash of health-related problems. "I am very pore & weak for want of Sufficient food," wrote Clark. Others suffered from "violent Coalds &

Strains," "tumers," "biles," dysentary, "cholick," "obstinate" coughs, fevers, "enfluenzy," rheumatism, and "looseness and gripeing." "We have not had as many sick at any one time since we left Wood River," reported Lewis in January 1806.[14]

One specific ailment plagued numerous members of the party, and it had nothing to do with weather or diet. "Goodrich has recovered from the Louis veneri which he contacted from an amorous contact with a Chinnook damsel," reported Lewis. "I cured him as I did Gibson last winter by the uce of murcury." Four days later Lewis ruefully "discovered that McNeal had the pox." The captains blamed the syphilis outbreak on young Indian women, who "Sport openly with our men."[15] But clearly the sporting fever was mutual.

Sex was a problem on the Columbia, not because of unavailability but of consequences. Native women communicated "venerious and pustelus disorders." They offered sex freely. William Clark explained: "Several Indians and Squars came this evening I beleave for the purpose of gratifying the passions of our men," he wrote early on. "Those people appear to View Sensuality as a necessary evile, and do not appear to abhore this as Crime in the unmarried females." The captains' proper behavior displeased everyone—"the female part appeared to be highly disgusted at our refuseing to axcept of their favours." In plain terms, "The *Chin nook* womin are lude and Carry on Sport publickly." After a winter at Fort Mandan, Lewis still did not understand the cultural significance of interracial sex. It cemented friendship, implied equality, and exchanged knowledge and power. "They do not hold the virtue of their women in high estimation," Lewis judged, "and will even prostitute their wives and daughters."[16] His attitude undoubtedly contributed to the winter's strained relationships. But the men were clearly not as fastidious, and Lewis beseeched them to abstain.

Meriwether Lewis spent most of his time at Fort Clatsop penning long, detailed, scientific descriptions of the local flora and fauna. This natural history record is ample recompense for the sentence of incarceration he endured. William Clark put the best light on his long, wet winter. "[A]t this place we had wintered and remained from the 7th of Decr. 1805 to this day," he wrote on his day of deliverance; "and have lived as well as we had any right to expect, and we can Say that we were never one day without 3 meals of Some kind a day either pore Elk meat or roots, not withstanding the repeated fall of rain which has fallen almost Constantly."[17]

Notes

1. *Journals,* V, 271, 288, October 14, 17, 1805 (Clark).

2. *Journals,* V, 311, 331, 333, 338, October 20, 24, 25, 1805 (Clark).

3. *Journals,* V, 335, October 24, 1805 (Clark).

4. *Journals,* V, 363, October 31, 1805 (Clark); VI, 19, November 4, 1805 (Clark).

5. *Journals,* VI, 33, 58, November 7, 1805 (Clark).

6. *Journals,* VI, 38, 75, November 9, 21, 1805 (Clark).

7. *Journals,* VI, 103, 107, December 1, 3, 1805 (Clark).

8. *Journals,* VI, 79, 92, 126, November 22, 28, December 16, 1805 (Clark).

9. *Journals,* VI, 32, 41, 76, November 7, 11, 21, 1805 (Clark); 436, March 19, 1806 (Lewis).

10. *Journals,* VI, 330–31, February 20, 1806 (Lewis); 123, 133–34, December 12, 20, 1805 (Clark); 164–65, January 4, 1806 (Lewis).

11. *Journals,* VI, 138, 139, December 25, 27, 1805 (Clark).

12. *Journals,* VI, 407, 410, March 12, 13, 1806 (Lewis); 147, December 31, 1805 (Clark).

13. *Journals,* VI, 36, 120, 122, 138, November 8, December 9, 12, 26, 1805 (Clark); 161, January 2, 1806 (Lewis).

14. *Journals,* VI, 181, 140, 122, 125, 135, 330, 336, January 8, 1806, December 28, 11, 14, 22 (Clark); February 20, 22, 1806 (Lewis).

15. *Journals,* VI, 239, 255, January 27, 31, 1806 (Lewis); 73, November 21, 1805 (Clark).

16. *Journals,* VI, 73, 136, 142, November 21, December 24, 29, 1805 (Clark); 168, January 6, 1806 (Lewis).

17. *Journals,* VII, 8, March 23, 1806 (Clark).

CHAPTER 5

HOMEWARD BOUND

With a sense of freedom and release the Corps of Discovery vacated Fort Clatsop on March 23, 1806. The weather, inclement as usual, had delayed departure. The captains had a strict schedule—to reach the Nez Perce by May 1, before those Indians left on a hunting expedition; to divide the Expedition and explore different routes through modern Montana; and to descend the Missouri before it iced up. They planned to be home before winter—and they made it.

The going was tough. The Columbia River, in spring runoff, was 20 feet higher in places and rapids were non-navigable. A reliable food supply was problematic; the men dried meat and bought dogs. Indians were "theives and scoundrels"; they stole tools, knives, and even Lewis's dog Seaman (he got it back). The Captain turned ruthless: "if they made any further attempts to steal our property or insulted our men we should put them to instant death." He would kill a man for a quip. His nerves were frayed. When he caught a native stealing an oar-lock he "gave him several severe blows," said he would "shoot the first of them that attempted to steal," and threatened "to kill them all" and "birn their houses."[1]

Following the south bank of the Columbia, Clark missed the mouth of the Willamette River again. It is hidden by Sauvie ("Image Canoe") Island. Retracing his steps from Sandy River on Indian advice, Clark explored the Willamette as far south as the site of modern Portland, Oregon.

The five canoes that left Fort Clatsop became battered, lost, and increasingly useless. Near The Dalles the captains began trading for horses, literally offering the clothes off their backs for overland transport. Eventually they acquired 23. Chief Yelleppit of the Walla Walla welcomed them with open arms and treated them to song and dance. From a few wandering Nez Perce they learned of an overland shortcut to the Clearwater, avoiding the Snake River and saving 80 miles. By early May, right on schedule, they were back with their old friends Tetoharsky and Twisted Hair in Nez Perce country. Most of their horses had survived the winter. A few had been misused. Chief Cutnose blamed Twisted Hair, but Clark forgave him. Twisted Hair's sons knew the way across the mountains.

Lewis and Clark were early. To their consternation, snow in the Bitterroot Mountains would remain too heavy for travel for more than a month. They set up camp on the Clearwater River and waited. Their layover was the longest of any except for the past three winters. Fortunately, the Nez Perce were clean, friendly, and helpful. The men engaged in recreational activities while William Clark administered to their physical ailments. A diet of dried fish and camas roots was supplemented with dogs, horses, and an occasional deer. Finally the captains could wait no longer. On June 10 they moved to the Weippe Prairie and on the 15th they attempted to cross the mountains without guides. Snow and cold defeated their efforts. Nine days later they tried again, this time with guides. Crusted snow held the horses, and they were back at Travellers Rest in six days. On the way they stopped for a hot bath at the Lolo Springs and ate a fresh deer-meat dinner. "This," recorded Clark, "is like once more returning to the land of the liveing."[2]

On July 3, at Travellers Rest, Lewis and Clark split up as per plan, not to be united for another six weeks. With a party of 23, including the Charbonneau family, Captain Clark returned to Ross's Hole and, bypassing the Shoshoni encampments on the Lemhi River, took a shortcut across Gibbon's Pass and through the Big Hole. He paused to test the hot springs near Jackson, marched down Grasshopper Creek, and headed, on Sacagawea's advice, to "Snake Indian cove" and the forks of the Beaverhead. Perhaps the expectation of the tobacco cached there spurred the smoke-starved men onwards. Recovering the canoes, a party under Sergeant Ordway made better time on the flooded Beaverhead and Jefferson Rivers than Clark did on horseback. He soon rejoined the river contingent for the trip "into that butifull and extensive Vally open and fertile which we Call the beaver head."[3] No more astonishing reversal of traveling conditions occurred than the trip downriver to Three Forks. In contrast to the laborious, meandering, 21-

day ascent of the previous August, the eastbound party once floated 90 miles in a day and completed the journey in three and a half days.

Nor did Clark's crew waste any time at Three Forks. Sergeant John Ordway immediately departed with nine men down the Missouri, to join forces with Sergeant Patrick Gass for the portage around the Falls. With 50 horses Clark and his reduced party took off up the beaver-choked Gallatin River. Sacagawea, "the indian woman who has been of great service to me as pilot through this country," pointed out Bozeman Pass, and on July 15 Clark struck the Yellowstone River.[4] Since there were no trees of sufficient size to hollow out for canoes, he kept on going, for five days and 100 miles. His horses went lame on the stone and gravel, so he had buffalo-skin "mockersons" made for them. On the 18th Private George Gibson fell and drove a snag deep into his thigh. He could neither walk nor ride, so canoes became imperative. Clark finally found two cottonwoods, which his men turned into 28-foot canoes, lashed together for stability. With this outrigger outfit, Clark's party set out on the river.

A successful canoe camp was fortunate, because one night Crow Indians stole half of Clark's horses. Sergeant Nathaniel Pryor took the rest on a quick overland trip to Fort Mandan. But on Pryor's second day out, he lost all of his mounts to the pilfering Crows. His party of four retreated to the Yellowstone, hastily built bullboats, and bobbed along some distance behind Clark.

Clark's group of nine descended the Yellowstone at prodigious rates of speed. In ten days it covered, by his generous estimation, nearly 650 miles. His exploration of the Yellowstone was necessarily brief and superficial. (Clark was unaware that the lower Yellowstone had been more thoroughly explored the year before by the British trader Francois Larocque.) On his second river day Clark climbed atop a massive sandstone rock, dubbed it "Pompy's Tower" in honor of Sacagawea's son, and carved his name on its side. The etching remains today—the only physical evidence anywhere of the Lewis and Clark Expedition.

Captain Clark saw so much game on the river—buffalo, elk, antelope, wolves—that he found it "incredituble" and resolved "to be silent on the Subject further." But the very next day he broke his promise, remarking on the "emence herds" he saw.[5] Once he lay for an hour while buffalo crossed the river. Near the Rosebud River he noted "Straters of Coal" in the streamcuts. He successfully negotiated (and named) the Wolf, Bear, and Buffalo Rapids. On August 3 he reached the

Missouri. His return from Travellers Rest lasted 32 days. The trip upriver between the same two points in 1805 had taken 134 days.

Meriwether Lewis, meanwhile, experienced a far more eventful return journey. With a party of nine he left Travellers Rest for the Clark Fork, where he and his men built three rafts to cross the river. His own sunk, and he reached the north shore swimming. The next day, the Fourth of July, his Nez Perce guides left him, fearful of following the "river of the road to Buffaloe" since it also led to the Blackfeet. Lewis took that road, through the "narrow confined pass" of Hellgate Canyon, up the "Cokahlahishkit" or Big Blackfoot River, and across the Continental Divide. He and his men celebrated their return to "the plains of the Missouri" by slaughtering a dozen buffalo. He turned north at the Dearborn River, reached the Sun River, and followed it to the Missouri and the old camp at White Bear Islands. He had come about 180 miles in nine days—a far cry from the 750 miles in 57 days in 1805.

The Great Falls caches had not fared well—Lewis lost his entire collection of Missouri River plants, painstakingly collected and pressed in 1805. Ten horses were missing one morning; Lewis feared they had been stolen. When Hugh McNeal survived an encounter with a grizzly, Lewis reflected "on a sertain fatality attatched to the neighbourhood."[6]

Lewis now embarked on the most inexplicable and foolhardy venture of the entire Expedition—a sojourn up the Marias River to "ascertain whether any branch of that river lies as far north as Lat.[d] 50."[7] Lewis had already hiked about sixty miles up the Marias the previous year and found that it flowed "too much to the North"; now he wanted to discover how much. The United States owned the entire Missouri River watershed; perhaps the Marias, a tributary of the Missouri, originated far enough to the north to infringe on British fur-trapping territory along the Athabaska and Saskatchewan Rivers in modern Canada.

With only three men—Drouillard and the Field brothers—and six horses, and with a scattered force at his back, Lewis ventured recklessly into territory inhabited by Indians he stigmatized as "a vicious lawless and reather an abandoned set of wretches." The Blackfeet had a reputation. This is the kind of situation Jefferson had envisioned when he cautioned Lewis against risking "probable destruction." "I wish to avoid an interview with them if possible," Lewis observed. "I have no doubt but they would steel our horses." Here was a self-fulfilling prophecy. Lewis knew what he was getting into.

For six days the men traveled north by northwest, "through wide and level plains which have somewhat the appearance of an ocean." Striking the Marias, they followed it and its tributary Cut Bank Creek for a hundred miles, to a point "about 10 miles below the foot of the rocky Mountains," where Lewis "lost all hope of the waters of this river ever extending to N Latitude 50°."[8] The headwaters emerged from the Rockies far to the south of Lewis's dream.

"Camp Disappointment," the northernmost point reached by the Expedition, reflected Lewis's attitude on realizing the Marias did not provide access to the Canadian fur trade, as well as the four days he spent unsuccessfully attempting under cloudy skies to ascertain longitude. "I now begin to be apprehensive that I shall not reach the United States within this season," he allowed.[9] He was in no mood to dally when, on his return to the Missouri, on the banks of Two Medicine Creek, he accomplished what he most hoped to avoid—an encounter with a band of Blackfeet Indians.

Lewis was spoiling for a fight. "I was convinced they would attempt to rob us," he stated, promising that "I should resist to the last extremity prefering death to that of being deprived of my papers instruments and gun." "In the loss of yourselves," Jefferson had cautioned, "we should lose also the information you will have acquired."[10]

The Blackfeet Lewis met were eight teenage boys, an advance unit of a much larger party a day-and-a-half's ride away. Lewis seized the initiative. He bestowed tokens of friendship on the three chiefs among them, discovered that they traded with the British on the Saskatchewan River and that there was a white man in the main camp, and invited them to dine and camp with him on Two Medicine River. He posted continuous guard and stood the first watch himself. But his eternal vigilance failed.

The next morning Lewis awoke to sounds of a scuffle and to Drouillard's cry, "damn you let go my gun." The Blackfeet had seized his party's rifles. Already, while Lewis slept, Reuben Field had chased an Indian 50 or 60 paces from camp and stabbed him in the heart. Lewis jumped up and, with the help of the Field brothers, recovered his gun. He forbade both the Fields and Drouillard from shooting the Indians; indeed, he might have allowed the Blackfeet to escape had they not attempted to scatter his horses. Two Medicine River was a long way from home without transportation. "I now hollowed to the men and told them to fire on them if they attempted to drive off our horses." The party divided: the men pursued six Indians who were taking most of the horses upriver; Lewis set out after two. "I pursued them so closely that they could not take twelve of their own horses but continued to drive one of mine." The captain chased them 300 paces until he was winded and they were cornered, warned them "that I would shoot them if they did not give me my horse," raised his gun, and shot one in the belly from a distance of 30 paces. The dying Indian returned the fire: "being bear headed I felt the wind of his bullet very distinctly." Then Lewis "returned leasurely towards camp." He did not retrieve his horse.

The Fields and Drouillard packed up three of the Expedition's horses and four of the best Indian mounts. Lewis retrieved a flag and burned shields, bows, and arrows, "but left the medal about the neck of the dead man that they might be informed who we were." The three men then beat a hasty retreat from Two Medicine River. "Having no doubt but that they would pursue us with a large party," they covered 100 miles before camping, pausing only to graze the horses. "My indian horse carried me very well," Lewis rationalized, "in short much better than my own would have done and leaves me with but little reason to complain of the robery."[11]

Lewis wrote his account of the fatal meeting some time afterwards, and he naturally put the best light on the proceedings. But he left a number of questions unanswered: why he ventured into hostile territory with only three men and a scattered force at his back; why he tarried in enemy country; why he deliberately antagonized his guests by telling them he had united their enemies in peace and trade (Blackfeet supremacy on the plains stemmed from the trade guns the group had recently acquired); why he posted only one watch over Indians he had predicted would rob him; why he pursued two Indians who had one of his horses when he had twelve of theirs; how he could warn his quarry that he would shoot them when he was running "nearly out of breath" and could not speak their language; why he fired first without apparent provocation; and why he treated the only known murders on the entire Expedition so cavalierly.

Blackfeet reaction to the killings is unknown. Whether the tribe excused the murders, since it was improper to rob visitors with whom they had smoked a pipe, or whether it descended to the Missouri in force, looking for the intruders, is conjectural. The death of He-that-looks-at-the-Calf and his companion, while not the sole cause, certainly helped to poison Blackfeet-American relations for the rest of the century. In sharp contrast to his meetings with Shoshoni, Flatheads, and Nez Perce, Lewis's interview with the Blackfeet proved tragic and portentous.

Still haunted by danger and ready to "wrisk our lives," the four men reached the Missouri early on the morning of July 28. There they fortuitously encountered Sergeant Ordway's canoe detail, coming down from the Falls. They abandoned their horses and took to the river. Lewis's mishaps were not yet over. Most of the items in the Marias caches were water-damaged, including "two very large bear skins which I much regret." The red pirogue had decayed beyond repair. The men all clambered aboard the canoes and headed downriver. They covered nearly 750 miles to the confluence with the Yellowstone in just 11 days—a marked reversal of their 36-day upstream journey of 1805. And they stopped to dry skins on August 2! As Lewis put it, "we are all extreemly anxious to reach the entrance of the Yellowstone."[12]

The Missouri return is noted chiefly for the wanton slaughter of game. In 11 days the hunters killed more than 120 animals, including over 60 deer, 23 elk, and 20 bighorns—more than one animal per man per day. "Game is so abundant and gentle that we kill it when we please," Lewis noted.[13] He even shot at bears from his canoe. He was the West's first slob hunter.

Lewis's party arrived at the Yellowstone on August 7. Clark's group, tormented by mosquitoes, had already gone downstream. Four days later Pierre Cruzatte, blind in one eye and near-sighted in the other, mistook Captain Lewis for an elk and shot him in the behind. On August 12 the Expedition, separated since Travellers Rest and divided at different times into five smaller parties, was at last reunited. Their combined exploits add up to a formidable geographic achievement.

Already Lewis and Clark had run into the first of nearly a dozen parties of fur traders coming upriver in 1806. Joseph Dickson and Forrest Hancock, two Illinoisans, returned to Fort Mandan with the explorers and persuaded Lewis to release John Colter from the U.S. Army. Three days at the Mandan villages was like old home time with the Hidatsa chief Le Borgne and the Mandans' Black Cat and Sheheke' ("Big White"). Sheheke agreed to visit Washington. The fort had burned, the Hidatsa had attacked the Shoshoni, and the Sioux and

Arikara were on the warpath. Lewis and Clark had preached peace, but not much changed.

Thirty-seven days after saying goodbye to the Mandans, the Lewis and Clark Expedition docked for the last time, at St. Louis. (The same trip upriver had taken 166 days!) Sometimes floating 75 miles in a day, there was little time for cordialities. They shook hands with the Arikaras, rowed right past the Sioux, smoked with the Yanktons, and repaired Sergeant Floyd's grave. They met old army men and acquaintances from 1804 like Joseph Gravelines and Pierre Dorion. They caught up on the news. Cows at La Charette meant civilization. They passed St. Charles, then Wood River, and finally reached St. Louis. On September 23, 1806, after 863 days, the journey was over.

Notes

1. *Journals,* VII, 104–5, 152, 156, April 11, 21, 22 1806 (Lewis).
2. *Journals,* VIII, 77, July 1, 1806 (Clark).
3. *Journals,* VIII, 175, July 10, 1806 (Clark).
4. *Journals,* VIII, 180, July 13, 1806 (Clark).
5. *Journals,* VIII, 219, 225, July 24, 25, 1806 (Clark).
6. *Journals,* VIII, 85, 88, 97, 110, July 3, 4, 8, 15, 1806 (Lewis).
7. *Journals,* VIII, 74, July 1, 1806 (Lewis).
8. *Journals,* VIII, 112–13, 123, July 17, 22, 1806 (Lewis).
9. *Journals,* VIII, 127, July 25, 1806 (Lewis).
10. *Journals,* VIII, 129, July 26, 1806 (Lewis); Jefferson's Instructions (Document 1).
11. *Journals,* VIII, 133–36, July 27, 1806 (Lewis).
12. *Journals,* VIII, 137, 146, July 28, August 2, 1806 (Lewis).
13. *Journals,* VIII, 149, August 6, 1806 (Lewis).

CHAPTER 6

SCIENCE AND ETHNOLOGY

The Lewis and Clark Expedition was conceived in the spirit of the 18th-century Enlightenment. The Enlightenment, or Age of Reason, was an Atlantic intellectual movement that stressed order, rationality, scientific exactitude, and the regularity and harmony of nature. Its American exemplars were Benjamin Franklin, Thomas Jefferson, and the Philadelphia scientific circle of Benjamin Rush, Benjamin Smith Barton, and Charles Willson Peale, which helped Meriwether Lewis prepare for the Expedition. Scientifically, the Enlightenment emphasized the collection and classification of the earth's plants and animals, as well as an explanation of its natural and physical wonders. Evidence and proof were its cardinal tenets and discovery and documentation its highest priorities.

Lewis and Clark were the Enlightenment's advance agents in the American West. Their duties, as assigned by Jefferson, were preeminently scientific—to explore, to discover, to "take careful observations," "to inform yourself, by inquiry, of the character & extent of the country," to acquire knowledge.[1] Specifically, they were instructed in geography, astronomy, ethnology, climatology, mineralogy, meteorology, botany, ornithology, and zoology. Neither Lewis nor Clark was a trained scientist. But most scientists in Jeffersonian America were not trained in the modern sense. Rather, they absorbed and exemplified the spirit of the age—the spirit of inquiry, of observation, of disciplined curiosity. Two incidents on the Expedition illustrate the Enlightenment's mania for information, for factual detail. When Lewis killed a rattlesnake on the Missouri, he dutifully reported that "it had 176 scuta on the abdomen and 25 on the tail." That is morbid fascination with a dead rattlesnake. And when the Shoshoni landed a mess of steelhead with a bush drag, Lewis counted them—all 528 of them.[2]

The Lewis and Clark Expedition was therefore a botanical expedition. The explorers discovered and described some 178 new plants, flowers, shrubs, grasses, and trees between St. Louis and the Pacific. Most of these new additions to scientific knowledge were found west of the Continental Divide, during the Expedition's lengthy sojourns at Fort Clatsop and Camp Chopunnish. Indeed, almost one-third, 55 to be exact, were located in modern Idaho. Several now bear the names of their discoverers. Among these are Lewis's wild flax (*Linum lewisii*), Lewis's monkey flower (*Mimulus lewisii*), and Lewis's syringa (*Philadelphus lewisii*). *Synthyris missurica* is popularly known as Lewis and Clark's synthyris. The Montana state flower, first uncovered on the morning of July 1, 1806, at the mouth of Lolo Creek, is *Lewisia rediviva*, the rockrose, or bitterroot.[3]

Some well-known trees first described by Lewis and Clark include three maples, three alders, two birches, two spruces (Engelmann and Sitka), and four pines (whitebark, lodgepole, western white, and ponderosa).

Most amazing are two plants first encountered in times of crisis. The white-margined spurge appeared on July 28, 1806—the same day that found Lewis in headlong retreat from the Blackfeet on Two Medicine Creek. And on August 12, 1806, when Lewis was suffering severe pain from a gunshot wound and "wriahting" was "extreemly painful" (it was the last day he would keep his journals), he could not resist noticing "a singular Cherry" on the Missouri River.

The Corps of Discovery lived off the land in the West, but also out of the water. Private Silas Goodrich was the Expedition's premier fisherman, and on June 13, 1805, the day Lewis discovered the Great Falls of the Missouri, he hooked the Enlightenment's first cutthroat trout, with its deep black specks, "long sharp teeth," and "a small dash of red on each side behind the front ventral fins." Once called *Salmo clarkii*, the cutthroat is now known as *Salar lewisii*. Other fishes new to science included the white sturgeon, which can grow to 20 feet, weigh 600 pounds, and live for 100 years; the channel catfish, which lent its name to the Expedition's first diplomatic parley with Indians at Camp White Catfish; the eulachon, or candlefish, so oily it burns like a taper; and the steelhead, described confusingly but accurately as the "steelhead salmon trout." Once classified as a salmon variety, the steelhead is now officially a trout.

Reptiles encountered by Lewis and Clark include the prairie rattlesnake, the bull snake, and the western garter snake. Turtles, frogs, toads and lizards round out the list.

Ornithology was the great avocation of early American science. Prominent bird collectors like Charles Willson Peale, Alexander Wilson, and Thomas Jefferson himself were associated with the Expedition of Lewis and Clark and anxiously awaited its feathered finds. The explorers did not disappoint their friends. They counted 51 birds new to science. Most distinctive are Lewis's woodpecker (*Asyndesmus lewis*), discovered on the Missouri River on July 20, 1805, and Clark's nutcracker, spotted on the Lemhi River on August 22, 1805.

A wide variety of other birds fills out the roster—ducks, geese, owls, grouse, hawks, crow, gulls, jays. On the West Coast Reuben Field killed a "buzzard," probably a California condor, with a wingspan of nine and a half feet and a body three feet, ten and a half inches long.

Larger mammals also greeted Lewis and Clark. Skunks, rabbits, packrats, ground squirrels, prairie dogs, and porcupines were amusing varieties new to science, as were the swift fox, the mountain sheep, the moose, the pronghorn (*Antelope americana*), and the western badger. One large animal, however, quickly captured the explorers' attention. The grizzly bear (*Ursus horribilis horribilis*) introduced itself at last to Meriwether Lewis and came to occupy more space in his journals than any other creature. Far down the Missouri he had listened incredulously to Indian reports of the great white bear. So fearsome was it that it took no fewer than 10 hunters to bring it down. Increasingly after Fort Mandan he had spotted tracks and other signs along the river. Now he was "anxious to meet with some of these bear," since "the Indians give a very formidable account of the strength and ferocity of this animal."[4]

Disappointingly, the first few grizzlies spotted by the Expedition quickly scurried off. Soon, however, they ran the other way—they charged. On April 29, 1805, Lewis shot one that "pursued me seventy or eighty yards." Though he was astonished at "the wounds they will bear before they can be put to death," he was not yet suitably impressed. "In the hands of skillfull riflemen," he boasted, "they are by no means as formidable or dangerous as they have been represented." Six days later, however, he marvelled at a grizzly bear that took 10 shots, including 5 through the lungs, to bring down, and he admitted "that the curiosity of our party is pretty well satisfyed with rispect to this anamal." And when a single bear scattered six hunters, driving two of them off a 20-foot cliff into the Missouri and diving in after them, Lewis was persuaded. Thereafter he wrote admiringly of "the farocity of those tremendious anamals"; he sent hunters out only in pairs; and when a grizzly chased him into the Missouri River near Great Falls, he could only wonder why fate had spared him.[5]

Medical prowess in Jefferson's America is epitomized by Benjamin Franklin's gibe that whenever he saw two physicians together, he looked up to watch the buzzards congregate. Doctors were a last resort; only when patients were at death's door did they call upon one to pull them through. It is hardly surprising, then, that the Lewis and Clark Expedition did not burden itself with the services of a physician. All illnesses were thought to originate in bad bodily fluids. The heroic remedies of the day—purges, bleedings, emetics, and cathartics—could be administered by anyone, and if one cure failed any other might suffice. Lewis's knowledge of medicine, acquired from his mother, a reputable herbalist, and from Dr. Benjamin Rush, the early republic's premier physician, together with his *materia medica* purchased in Philadelphia, constituted the Expedition's only defense against illness and injury. Systematically administered throughout the West, Dr. Lewis's patients survived despite his ministrations.[6]

Routine ailments plagued the corps. Icy rivers, diet deficiencies, sharp stones and prickly pear, and the steady strain of hard physical labor caused accidents, rheumatism, dysentery, boils, "tumers," and fevers. Glauber salts, a laxative; laudanum, a solution of opium in alcohol; and frequent bleedings somehow brought relief, if not cures. Benjamin Rush, a phlebotomist, once recommended that up to three-quarters of a patient's blood supply be removed. Relaxation, he noted surprisingly, was immediate! Lewis once bled Joseph Whitehouse "plentifully" with his penknife; "it answered very well."[7]

Four major medical problems marked the passage through the West. One was Sergeant Charles Floyd's illness and death, presumably from a ruptured appendix. Another was Sacagawea's sickness at the Marias River (described in her biography). Two others afflicted the captains themselves. Meriwether Lewis, walking to the Great Falls in June 1805, was suddenly seized with "violent pain in the intestens" and high fever. He boiled chokecherry twigs in water "untill a strong black decoction of an astringent bitter tast was produced." Two pints at hour intervals brought a miraculous recovery; the next day he hiked 27 miles.[8]

William Clark arrived at the Three Forks in July 1805 feeling fatigued, feverish, bilious, and constipated. He revealed to Lewis that he "had not had a passage for several days." Lewis prescribed five of Dr. Rush's "bilious pills," a laxative so powerful the pills were known as "Rush's Thunderbolts." Clark spent an extremely restless night, but he was up and about the next day.[9] In both cases, recovery was a tribute to the medicine and to the patient's constitution.

One other medical saga played out on the Columbia River. At Fort Clatsop Private William Bratton suffered from severe lower-back pains so debilitating he could barely walk. Lewis thought he might die. He traveled upriver in boats and on horseback. At Camp Chopunnish, he tried an Indian sweat bath. Naked, he sat inside a covered pit and sprinkled water on red-hot rocks. After 45 minutes he plunged into an icy stream. He repeated the treatment. He recovered fully for the rest of the trip and never, apparently, suffered a relapse.[10]

Thomas Jefferson's instructions to Meriwether Lewis were explicitly geographical. "The object of your mission," he wrote in his first real command, "is to explore the Missouri river, & such principal stream of it, as, by it's course and communication with the waters of the Pacific ocean, whether the Columbia, Oregan, Colorado or any other river may offer the most direct & practicable water communication across this continent for the purposes of commerce." He continued: "The interesting points of the portage between the heads of the Missouri, & of the water offering the best communication with the Pacific ocean, should also be fixed by observation."[11] Clearly Jefferson believed that a "direct & Practicable water communication" existed out West, perhaps with a "fixed" portage. He believed in a Northwest Passage.[12]

Herein lies the heart and soul of the voyage of discovery—the search for a waterway across the North American continent. From the time of Christopher Columbus the quest for such a passage had inspired generations of explorers. But the West of Jefferson's imagination clashed with the reality of the Rocky Mountains. Lewis and Clark laid the issue, once for all, to rest. There was no northwest passage, only "those tremendious mountains." Yet Lewis could not let go. He tried desperately to put the best light on his failure to find a nonexistent passage. "We have discovered," he boldly affirmed, "the most practicable rout which dose exist across the continent by means of the navigable branches of the Missouri and Columbia Rivers." So far, so good. But then Lewis described a "passage by land of 340 miles from the Missouri to the Kooskooske [Clearwater River]" as "the most formidable part of the tract." Uh-oh. "[O]f this distance," he explained, "200 miles is along a good road, and 140 over tremendious mountains which for 60 mls. are covered with eternal snows." To equate an arduous, mountainous crossing of 340 miles with a practicable and navigable passage is an intellectual act of faith. Not even the most sanguine navigator could cling any longer to the dream of a "direct and practicable water communication across this continent."[13]

Lewis's route was not even the shortest and fastest path to the Pacific. A succeeding generation headed up the Platte River and across South Pass in Wyoming on the wagon trail to Oregon. A paved road over Lolo Pass did not exist until 1962.

President Jefferson also told Lewis to learn all he could about Native Americans in the West. Along the Missouri and its headwaters these tribes would be living in American Louisiana, subject, presumably, to the sovereignty of the United States. Along the Columbia and its headwaters the tribes would be in foreign country. But all were subject to the captain's investigations.[14]

For the most part, the relationships of Lewis and Clark with the some three dozen Indian tribes they encountered were highly successful. The Expedition moved deliberately up the Missouri and down the Snake and Columbia Rivers, lived peaceably among the natives at Forts Mandan and Clatsop, and traded with almost everyone for foodstuffs and necessities. In particular, the Mandan, Shoshoni, and Nez Perce tribes were pivotal to the progress of the Corps of Discovery.

On the Missouri, the Teton Sioux were confrontational and the Hidatsa standoffish. But relations with the Oto, Missouri, Yankton Sioux, Arikara, and Mandan peoples were cordial and productive. Lewis and Clark proclaimed sovereignty, preached peace, promised protection, and promoted continued commerce. Often they did not recognize the realities of native culture, particularly the ritual nature of warfare—it served as a merit system for status and leadership—and the practice of adoption rites, whereby tribes might wage war during one season and do business the next. Indian cultures were more complex than Lewis and Clark realized. Moreover, promises of Jeffersonian paternalism proved impossible to keep, especially after the government's monopoly on trade ended in the 1820s. Unscrupulous gunrunners and whisky peddlers subverted rather than supported Indian societies. But Lewis and Clark may be pardoned for predicting a future that never came.

The Plateau tribes of the Rocky Mountains were critical, essential, to the progress and success of the Expedition. The Shoshoni, nervous and agitated throughout, nevertheless provided baggage handlers, horses, directions, and guides. At times Meriwether Lewis had to threaten or shame Cameahwait and his followers into carrying out the tasks he prescribed for them, but they always complied. The Flatheads parted with 13 horses. Without the Nez Perce, the Expedition might never have made it. Had they been at all hostile, the men, sick to death on the Weippe Prairie, would have been easy pickings. But the Nez Perce nursed them back to relative health, showed them how to build canoes, took care of their horses, and sent Twisted Hair and Tetoharsky all the way to The Dalles to make introductions. The Rockies confounded the Expedition; the Shoshoni and Nez Perce helped overcome them.

On the Snake and Columbia Rivers, Lewis and Clark were in a different, foreign country. It might have helped had they preferred salmon to dog for dinner; perhaps they would have fit better into the fish-and-trade river culture. The Wanapams and the Yakimas at the mouth of the Snake were friendly enough, as were the Walulas (Walla Wallas) of Chief Yelleppit. All staged ceremonial welcomes for the Expedition. But the Umatillas, who had never seen a white person, were scared and hostile. When Clark nonchalantly shot a crane out of the sky, they cowered in their huts.

Approaching The Dalles, Lewis and Clark increasingly encountered European clothing and trade goods. They were at the commercial center of the inland empire, on the border of Sahaptian (west) and Chinookan (east) linguistic regions, amid large numbers of Wishram ("Echeloots") and Wasco Indians. Theft was a problem. Indians helped themselves to the Expedition's loose goods, in unauthorized return for assistance or simply as a statement of their importance. The Americans became increasingly wary and even resentful. The Skilloots, near the mouth of the Willamette, must have reminded Lewis and Clark of the Teton Sioux. Powerful middlemen, they made themselves assertive and disagreeable. No way the Expedition would winter among these people.

Lewis and Clark did not like the looks or the trading practices of the Chinooks and the Cathlamets on the north shore of the Columbia estuary. They were more than happy to relocate among the Clatsops, with whom they maintained a winter of armed formality. Clatsop visits to the Fort were few, unappreciated, and rarely reciprocated. Sentries closed the gates at 6:00 P.M. and expelled visitors. The Clatsops had no need for the Expedition's pathetic supply of trade goods. White men, and even black, were not curiosities. The captains sneered at Clatsop appearances, head-pressing customs, and sexual practices. They did admire local rain gear and ordered a couple of conical woven hats for themselves. Mainly, however, they waited out the winter in splendid isolation.

The Clatsops crafted fine oceangoing canoes, capable of cutting easily through high winds and waves. Lewis coveted one. When Chief Coboway refused to sell, he stole it. The incident illustrates the low level of intercultural relations during the long Clatsop winter.

The Lewis and Clark Expedition did not occur in a vacuum. The West was not an empty wilderness, to be overcome or "opened." The American West was occupied territory, and to pass through it Lewis and Clark needed Indian cooperation, assistance, and sustenance. Without Native Americans the Corps of Discovery would have starved to death along the way or gotten hopelessly lost in the Rockies. To the names of Meriwether Lewis, William Clark, and the others, let us add individuals of equal importance to the Expedition's success—Sheheke, Le Borgne, Cameahwait, Old Toby, Twisted Hair, Yelleppit, and Coboway. And their people. And Sacagawea, who represents them all.

Notes

1. Jefferson's Instructions to Lewis, 20 June 1803, *Letters of the Lewis and Clark Expedition, with Related Documents, 1783–1854,* ed. Donald Jackson, 2 vols. (Urbana: University of Illinois Press, 1978), I, 61–66.

2. *Journals,* VIII, 147, August 4, 1806; V, 144, August 22, 1805 (Lewis).

3. The indispensable source for the Expedition's scientific discoveries is Paul Russell Cutright, *Lewis and Clark: Pioneering Naturalists* (1969; reprint, Lincoln: University of Nebraska Press, 1989).

4. *Journals,* IV, 31, April 13, 1805 (Lewis).

5. *Journals,* IV, 84–85, 113, 118, 141, April 29, May 5, 6, 11, 1805 (Lewis).

6. See, generally, Eldon G. Chuinard, *Only One Man Died: The Medical Aspects of the Lewis and Clark Expedition* (Glendale, Calif.: A. H. Clark Co., 1979) and David J. Peck, *Or Perish in the Attempt: Wilderness Medicine in the Lewis and Clark Expedition* (Helena, Mont.: Farcountry Press, 2002).

7. *Journals,* IV, 334, June 26, 1805 (Lewis).

8. *Journals,* IV, 278, June 11, 1805 (Lewis).

9. *Journals,* IV, 436, July 27, 1805 (Lewis); 438, July 27, 1805 (Clark).

10. *Journals,* VII, 282–83, May 24, 1806 (Lewis).

11. Jefferson's Instructions to Lewis, 20 June 1803, *Letters,* I, 61–66.

12. The essential source for geographical information is John Logan Allen, *Passage through the Garden: Lewis and Clark and the Image of the American Northwest* (Urbana: University of Illinois Press, 1975).

13. Lewis to Jefferson, 23 September 1806, *Letters,* I, 320.

14. The paramount study is James P. Ronda, *Lewis and Clark among the Indians* (Lincoln: University of Nebraska Press, 1984). See also Ronda, "Lewis & Clark and Enlightenment Ethnography," in William F. Willingham and Leonoor Swets Ingraham, eds., *Enlightenment Science in the Pacific Northwest: The Lewis and Clark Expedition* (Portland, Ore.: Lewis and Clark College, 1984), 5–17.

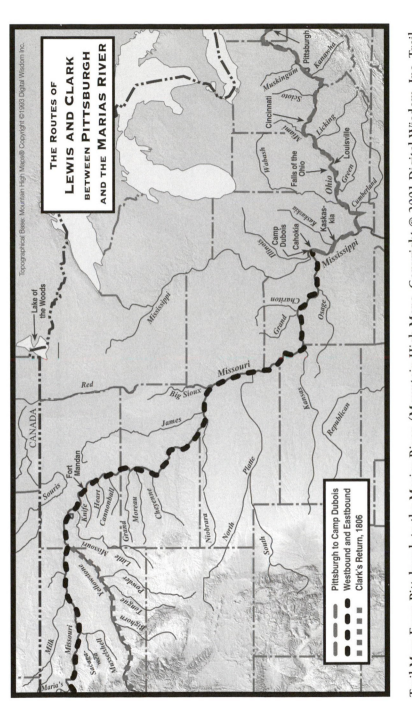

Trail Map: From Pittsburgh to the Marias River. (Mountain High Maps, Copyright © 2001 Digital Wisdom, Inc. Trail information added by Joseph A. Mussulman.)

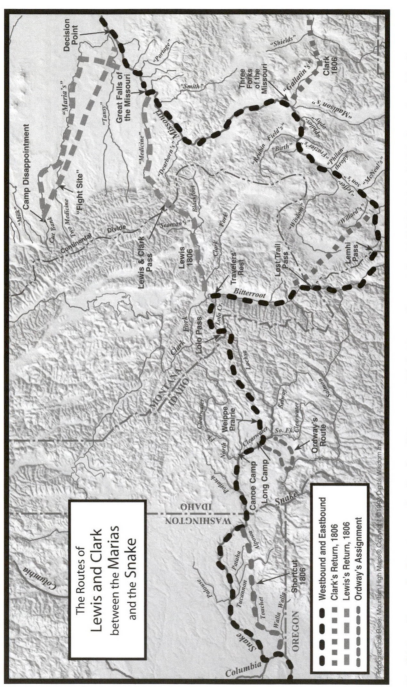

Trail Map: From the Marias to the Snake. (Mountain High Maps, Copyright © 2001 Digital Wisdom, Inc. Trail information added by Joseph A. Mussulman.)

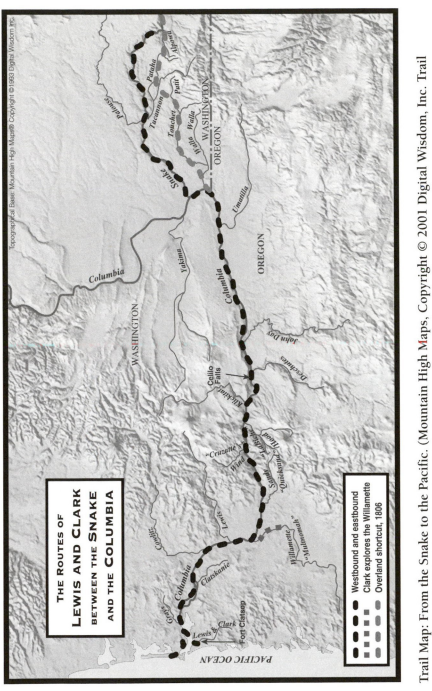

Trail Map: From the Snake to the Pacific. (Mountain High Maps, Copyright © 2001 Digital Wisdom, Inc. Trail information added by Joseph A. Mussulman.)

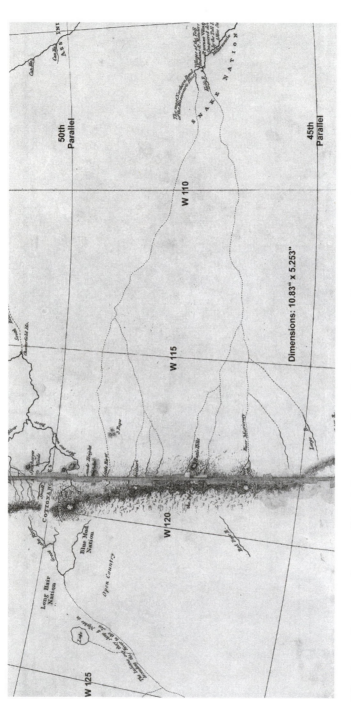

The Aaron Arrowsmith map of 1802 depicts no obstacles between the Missouri and the Pacific. (Map Division, Library of Congress.)

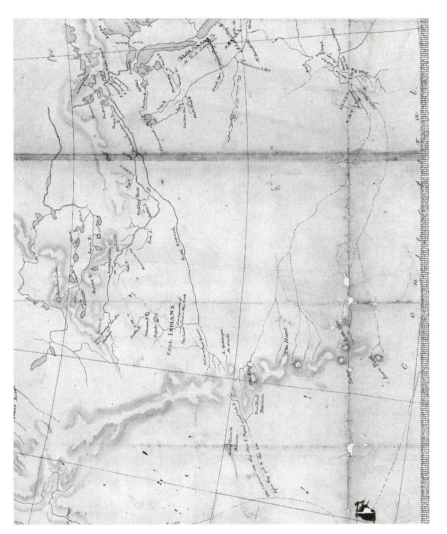

Nicholas King's map of 1803 shows the Rockies as a single chain. (Map Division, Library of Congress.)

William Clark's 1805 map is the first accurate depiction of the Missouri. (Map Division, Library of Congress.)

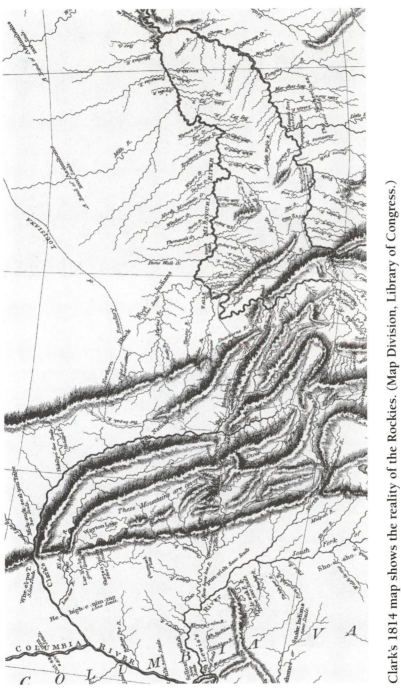

Clark's 1814 map shows the reality of the Rockies. (Map Division, Library of Congress.)

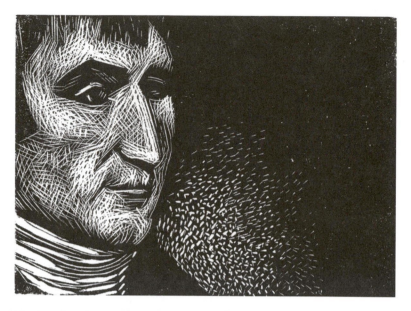

Meriwether Lewis. (Wood engraving by James Todd.)

William Clark. (Wood engraving by James Todd.)

Sacagawea, on the U.S. Dollar. (U.S. Mint.)

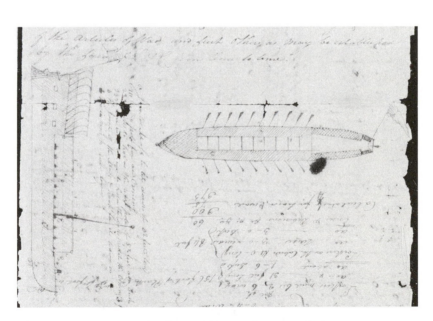

Clark's drawing of the keelboat. (Yale Collection of Western Americana, Beinecke Rare Book and Manuscript Library.)

The White Cliffs of the wild and scenic Missouri. (© Joseph Mussulman/VIAs, Inc.)

The Great Falls of the Missouri. (A. E. Mathews, *Pencil Sketches of Montana* [New York: self-published, 1868].)

(left) The Montana State Flower, *Lewisia rediviva*, the rock rose, or bitterroot. (Mark Behan/VIAs, Inc.)

(below) Beacon Rock, on the Columbia River. (E. G. Chuinard/Lewis and Clark Trail Heritage Foundation. Print used with permission of the Lewis and Clark Trail Heritage Foundation, Inc. Taken by Frenchy Chuinard, Past President LCTHF.)

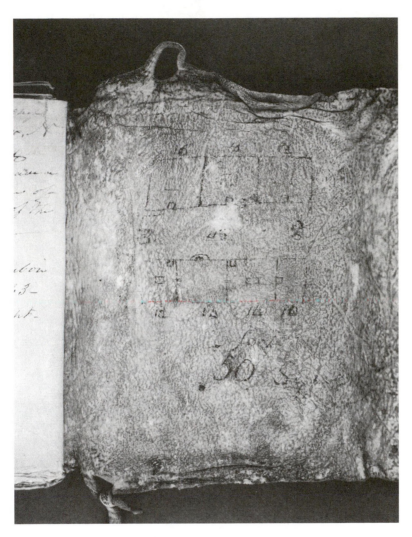

Fort Clatsop floor plan. (Missouri Historical Society.)

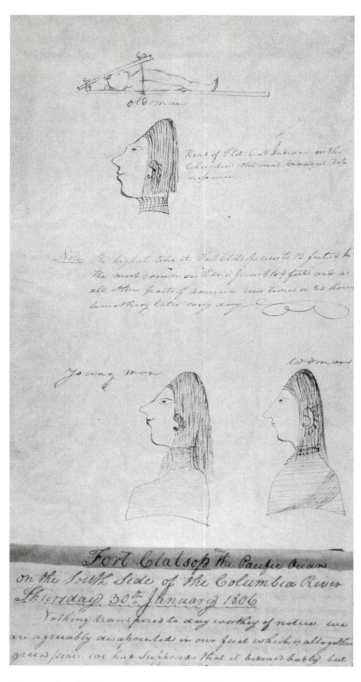

Clatsop head flattening. (Missouri Historical Society.)

Clatsop hat. (Allan McMakin/VIAs, Inc.)

Eulachon, or candlefish. (Missouri Historical Society.)

Pompey's Pillar, on the Yellowstone River. (Montana Historical Society, No. 950–257.)

Clark's signature on Pompey's Pillar. (Montana Historical Society, No. 950–262.)

CHAPTER 7

EPILOGUE

The Lewis and Clark Expedition had relatively little impact, in either the short or the long run, upon American destiny. Upon their return to the East in 1806, the captains were feted as heroes, as symbols of national optimism and pride. Other government-sponsored exploration parties, even to the moon and Mars, are part of their legacy. But America's future would have transpired pretty much as it did if the Lewis and Clark Expedition had never occurred. The era of the Far Western fur trade, as much exploration as economics, began even before Lewis and Clark finished their work. Astoria (John Jacob Astor's trading post on the Columbia River estuary in 1811), Indian removal, and the Oregon Trail were in America's cards. Lewis and Clark exemplified what one historian calls "republican nationalism"—a sense of limitless American possibilities and opportunities.[1] They were just one example.

As the 19th century wore on, the reputation of Lewis and Clark and knowledge of their achievements faded from national memory. The rapid pace of time and progress eclipsed their accomplishments. Others reaped renown and fortune from exploration and exploitation of the West. On some counts, such as Lewis's claim to "have discovered the most practicable rout" across the continent, they were spectacularly wrong. Humanitarian policies governing Indian trade and protection yielded abruptly to private enterprise and private greed. At century's end, Lewis and Clark were trailblazers but little more.

The main problem was lack of an evidentiary record. History is not the past, it is the record of the past, and although Lewis and Clark kept meticulous records and observations, most were unknown and unavailable. Thomas Jefferson believed that the original journals of the Expedition were government property, but he expected Lewis and

Clark to publish them privately. Lewis made the necessary arrangements, but he never submitted a single line to press. He wrote a prospectus (an advertisement), hired a publisher, engaged artists to illustrate his work, consulted naturalists and mathematicians—and never wrote a word.[2] Meriwether Lewis suffered the most debilitating case of writer's block in American history.

Lewis's papers from the Pacific were with him when he took his own life in Tennessee on October 11, 1809. Miraculously, they did not perish with him. His traveling companion James Neelly sent them to Washington. William Clark picked them up there and took them to Philadelphia. Clark engaged Nicholas Biddle, a Federalist *litterateur,* as an editor. In 1814 Biddle issued a two-volume paraphrase as *The History of the Expedition.* The narrative omitted nearly all of the scientific data upon which the fame of Lewis and Clark now rests. Parts of it, dealing with sexual practices among Indians, appeared in Latin. Public interest, thanks to Zebulon Pike and the War of 1812, had shifted. The volumes sold poorly. Only two thousand were printed to begin with. Clark never made a dime; he did not even own a copy for over two years. With little to sustain it, the reputation of Lewis and Clark faded.

Nearly eight decades later, Elliott Coues, a surgeon and amateur naturalist, borrowed the original journals from the American Philosophical Society. He was astounded at the wealth of ethnological and biological information they contained. Coues's annotation of the Biddle edition (1893) first revealed to the public that the Expedition was something more than an extended hike. Finally, to mark the Expedition's centennial, Reuben Gold Thwaites of the Wisconsin Historical Society published for the first time all of the original journals of Lewis and Clark. The public now had an annotated abridgement and a relatively unglossed original. Another eight decades passed.

In the meantime, more Lewis and Clark material came to light. Thwaites found some, in the possession of Clark's descendants in St. Louis. Biddle's grandsons turned over John Ordway's journal and Lewis's Ohio "river journal" in 1913. Clark's field notes appeared in an attic in Minneapolis in 1953. The first calls for a comprehensive, documented edition sounded.

The last 50 years have witnessed a resounding Lewis and Clark revival. Bernard DeVoto launched it in 1953 with an abridged edition of Thwaite's original journals—a book still in print and selling well. Donald Jackson collected and printed over 400 letters and documents related to the Expedition. Major scholarly monographs interpreted the Expedition. With Paul Cutright on science, John Logan Allen on geography, and James Ronda on Native Americans, we now know more about the Expedition than its leaders did. Stephen Ambrose's stirring biography of Meriwether Lewis put the Expedition atop the best-seller charts.

The culmination of this enterprise is the magnificent 13-volume edition of *The Journals of the Lewis & Clark Expedition,* edited by Gary E. Moulton and published by the University of Nebraska Press (1983–2001). It is the standard reference for the 21st century. Lewis and Clark are now better known and more widely read than ever before. The Journals are their monument. Their reputation has never been higher. The Expedition is an American treasure.

Notes

1. J. William T. Youngs, "Republican Nationalism: The Lewis and Clark Expedition," *American Realities: Historical Episodes,* 4th ed., 2 vols. (New York: Longman, 1997), I, 135–55.

2. The fascinating account of the provenance of the writings of Lewis and Clark is told in Paul Russell Cutright, *A History of the Lewis and Clark Journals* (Norman: University of Oklahoma Press, 1976).

BIOGRAPHIES

Thomas Jefferson (April 2/13, 1743–July 4, 1826)

His obituary reads

THOMAS JEFFERSON
Author of the Declaration of American Independence,
Of the Statute of Virginia for
Religious Freedom,
and Father of the University of Virginia

Nothing of his political or diplomatic career, as delegate, governor, minister, secretary, vice president, and president. Nothing as statesman, scientist, architect, and "apostle of freedom and enlightenment." Nothing of Louisiana or Lewis and Clark. Jefferson's epitaph is the grossest understatement in American history.

He was born in Albemarle County, Virginia, to Peter and Jane (Randolph) Jefferson, a member from birth of a prominent family on the western edge of settlement. Something of a prodigy, he studied Latin and Greek before entering, in 1760, the College of William and Mary. Two years in Williamsburg opened him to politics, science, and society. Always a bookworm, he studied law (to make a living) and political theory (to argue against Britain). Both subjects served him well in the Virginia House of Burgesses (1769–1775), where he wrote *A Summary View of the Rights of British America* (1774), a revolutionary tract that antedated the Declaration of Independence by blaming the king for America's problems. Jefferson hated monarchs and monarchy. His colleagues recognized his literary talents, and he did not disappoint them.

In the Virginia House of Delegates (1776–1779) he opposed aristocracies of birth and wealth (but not of land) and supported measures promoting talent, liberty of conscience, and education. As governor of Virginia (1779–1781), however, constitutional limitations on his power hampered defensive preparations against British invasion. He recovered by writing *Notes on the State of Virginia* (1787), a strange but brilliant combination of statistical analysis and philosophical inquiry. After a stint in the Confederation Congress (1783–1784), where his land reports became the basis of the later Northwest Ordinance, he became minister to France (1784–1789). Jefferson loved Paris—its wine, women, and culture—but he professed that Europe strengthened his Americanness.

Except for a few years mid-decade, Jefferson spent the 1790s in public service, as secretary of state (1790–1793) under George Washington and vice president (1797–1801) under John Adams. He came to believe that the Federalists were monarchists, and he led the agrarian opposition to Alexander Hamilton's market republicanism. The Electoral College in 1797 chose Jefferson, a Democratic-Republican, to serve under Adams, a Federalist. In opposition to his own administration, he secretly wrote the Kentucky Resolution of 1798, which undermined the strength of Constitutional government. In 1801 he became president in his own right, after the House of Representatives broke an electoral tie with Aaron Burr.

Jefferson's two terms (1801–1809) are noted for strong presidential and party leadership, fiscal economy in a government of ostensibly limited powers, a knock-down battle with the Federalist judiciary, the purchase of Louisiana, and a growing crisis with Britain and France, highlighted by the Embargo Act of 1807. The president gladly handed his office to his protégé, James Madison, in 1809, and retired to Monticello, his hilltop Italianate mansion near Charlottesville.

It is impossible to sum up the life, achievements, and philosophy of Thomas Jefferson. He is a towering Enlightenment figure who spent his life, it seems, writing about everything. His published works, when completed, will fill a hundred thick volumes. But let us elaborate on three powerful themes.

1. Jefferson's timelessness, the Jefferson Memorial, rests on his unceasing advocacy of liberty and equality, of democracy and individual freedom. These truths are "self-evident," he wrote in the Declaration: "all men are created equal" and endowed with "certain unalienable rights . . . among these are life, liberty, and the pursuit of happiness."[1] This is what he wanted to be remembered for and have inscribed on his tombstone. He hated the artificial barriers of the past—aristocracy and "monkish ignorance and

superstition." In the last letter of his life (June 24, 1826) he expounded "the palpable truth, that the mass of mankind has not been born with saddles on their backs, nor a favored few booted and spurred, ready to ride them legitimately, by the grace of God."[2] These are American values, even today. James Parton summed up: "If Jefferson was wrong, America is wrong. If America is right, Jefferson was right."

2. Jefferson was a philosopher of agrarianism. "Those who labour in the earth are the chosen people of God . . . whose breasts he has made his peculiar deposit for substantial and genuine virtue . . . Corruption of morals in the mass of cultivators is a phaenomenon of which no age nor nation has furnished an example."[3] Jefferson believed in a nation of small farmers, owning enough land to guarantee economic self-sufficiency and personal independence. Land was the key to the republican experiment; "room enough for our descendants to the hundredth and thousandth generation," he said, even before the Louisiana Purchase, his finest achievement, added 15 million agricultural acres to the national domain.[4]

The necessity for land to sustain a fee-simple republic built in contradictions that not even Jefferson fully understood. It was imperialistic. Jefferson opposed urban manufacturing: "let our workshops remain in Europe . . . The mobs of great cities add just so much to the support of pure government, as sores do to the strength of the human body."[5] America would buy its manufactures from Europe, paying for them by selling surplus agricultural commodities. But a growing population meant more imports, more surpluses, and therefore more land. Jefferson bought Louisiana; his successors stole half of Mexico from their sister republic. "Manifest Destiny" was a conscious attempt to prolong the republican present and deny the industrial future.

Finally, new lands for farmers meant new lands for slaves. Jefferson's "Empire for Liberty" risked an "Empire for Slavery." Every sectional quarrel between the Revolution and the Civil War originated in the territories. When the Kansas-Nebraska Act (1854) opened land that Jefferson had bought to possible slavery expansion, the Jeffersonian conundrum had come full circle.

3. Jefferson loved the West. The front windows of Monticello faced the sunset. His Revolution acquired the Midwest; his administration purchased Louisiana; his successors grabbed California, the Southwest, and Oregon. Jefferson's desire to explore the West was long-standing. He talked to George Rogers Clark, John Ledyard, and André Michaux. Finally, he sent Lewis and Clark to the Pacific.

> I never saw it. As you know, I never crossed
> The mountains to Kentucky, and the West.
> But I had sent good Meriwether there,
> Across the plains and the last mountains, to the ocean,
> To name and chart, and set the human foot.
> But it was my West.
>
> Thomas Jefferson, in Robert Penn Warren,
> *Brother to Dragons.*

Thomas Jefferson died, providentially, on July 4, 1826, the 50th anniversary of his Declaration of Independence, and, coincidentally, on the same day as John Adams. Let us add one more line, Meriwether Lewis's line, to his epitaph: "the author of our enterprize, that illustrious personage, Thomas Jefferson."[6]

Meriwether Lewis (August 18, 1774–October 11, 1809)

Meriwether Lewis was born in Albemarle County, Virginia—Jefferson's county. The Lewises and the Jeffersons were not only neighbors but distant relatives. Indeed, the Virginia plantocracy has been described as one giant cousinage. "Meriwether" was his mother's maiden name. His father, William Lewis, served in the Continental Army during the American Revolution. He died in 1779. His mother Lucy soon remarried, to John Marks, another army veteran.

Marks moved his family, including Lewis's brother Reuben and two half-siblings, to a plantation in Georgia, near modern Athens. In the Piedmont hills of Virginia and on the Georgia frontier young Meriwether learned to hike and hunt. Back in Virginia at age 13 he learned math, science, and Latin from Matthew Maury, a private tutor. When John Marks died in 1792, Lucy returned to Charlottesville, and Meriwether managed her plantation.

So far Lewis was on track to become an active, literate member of the Virginia ruling classes. But when President George Washington called for troops to suppress the Whisky Rebellion in western Pennsylvania in 1794, Lewis, a member of his local militia, responded. He was "quite delighted with a soldier's life," he told his mother. It appealed to "this Quixottic disposition of mine."[7] So he enlisted in the regular army and began a career that carried him on official errands throughout the American Midwest and to the rank of captain with duties as a paymaster. He was present at Greenville, Ohio, in 1795, when General "Mad"

Anthony Wayne negotiated a treaty with the Miami and Shawnee Indians that secured most of the future state of Ohio to the American republic. He served at such outposts as Fort Pickering (Memphis) and Detroit.

Lewis was an ensign (a modern second lieutenant) in the U.S. 2nd Sub-Legion in 1795, serving under Lieutenant William Clark. The two men became fast friends and remained so, even after Clark resigned his commission and returned to private life in Kentucky.

When Thomas Jefferson became President in 1801, he needed a private secretary—not to take dictation or file papers but in a military capacity, as a courier or an aide-de-camp. "Your knolege of the Western country, of the army and of all it's interests," he told Lewis, make you the man for the job.[8] Lewis accepted and spent two years in Washington, living in the White House, conferring with the president, delivering messages, and making himself useful. One of his tasks was to grade the members of the army officer corps according to their Republicanism, so Jefferson would know who his political enemies were.

An early schoolmate later described Lewis as "always remarkable for perseverance which in the early period of his life seemed nothing more than obstinacy." He continued: Lewis had "a martial temper; great steadiness of purpose, self-possession, and undaunted courage."[9] This characterization was drawn from Thomas Jefferson's obituary of Lewis, published in 1814. "Of courage undaunted," Jefferson wrote,

> possessing a firmness & perserverance of purpose which nothing but impossibilities could divert from it's direction, careful as a father of those committed to his charge, yet steady in the maintenance of order & discipline . . . honest, disinterested, liberal, of sound understanding and a fidelity to truth.

"With all these qualifications," Jefferson concluded, "I could have no hesitation in confiding the enterprise to him."[10]

Yet there was another side to Lewis's character. He could be rash, even reckless. Jefferson's attorney general, Levi Lincoln of Massachusetts, pointed to this trait. "From my ideas of Capt. Lewis," he wrote, "he will be much more likely, in case of difficulty, to push too far, than to recede too soon." Jefferson agreed; he changed the word *certain* to *probable* in his instructions to Lewis: "We value too much the lives of citizens to offer them to probable destruction," he wrote.[11]

Manuel Lisa, a St. Louis fur trader and no friend of Lewis, considered him headstrong and imprudent. A modern psychologist believes that a life history of excessive risk taking stemmed from Lewis's early loss of his father.

Even less salutary traits appear in Jefferson's obituary of Lewis. "Governor Lewis had from early life," the former president wrote, "been subject to hypocondriac affections. It was a constitutional disposition in all the nearest branches of the family of his name, & was more immediately inherited by him from his father." *Hypocondria* meant a "morbid state of mind," melancholia, or low spirits. The modern term is "depression." Historians today believe Lewis suffered from clinical depression—manic, morbid, or mild. Jefferson said that when Lewis "lived with me in Washington, I observed at times sensible depressions of mind."

Earlier, Jefferson noted that Lewis "was much afflicted and habitually so with hypocondria. This was probably increased by the habit into which he had fallen."[12] The "habit" was intemperance. Lewis had a problem with alcohol. In 1795 he had been court-martialed for drunkenness and conduct unbecoming an officer. He took 120 gallons of distilled spirits up the Missouri River in 1804. Excessive drinking most assuredly contributed to his suicide in 1809.

Late in 1802 President Jefferson began contemplating a Missouri River exploration, and by February 1803 Meriwether Lewis was its leader. If we believe Jefferson, Lewis asked for the job and Jefferson gave it to him. Ten years earlier, Lewis had volunteered for the André Michaux party, and on the trail he once reflected that exploring the West had been his "darling project" for a decade.

The president's interests included natural science and ethnology, as well as exploration and empire, and by early 1803 Lewis was boning up on these subjects. He took crash courses in medicine from America's foremost physician, Benjamin Rush; in botany from the prominent scientist Benjamin Smith Barton; in zoology from Professor Caspar Wistar; and in celestial observation from the mathematician Robert Patterson. He traveled to Lancaster, Pennsylvania, and to Philadelphia for these lessons, and to pick up supplies and materials. He ordered weapons and the iron framework of a canoe from the federal armory at Harpers Ferry, Virginia. By the 4th of July in 1803 he was ready to go.

Lewis's reward for his successful transcontinental journey was an appointment as governor of Upper Louisiana, with headquarters in St. Louis. In retrospect, the job was his punishment as well. Lewis was a soldier, not a politician. Instinctively, he may have known that; he did not show up to assume his duties until March 8, 1808! By that time, he was in over his head. Unscrupulous associates, especially Territorial Secretary Frederick Bates, and uncooperative Indians, primarily the Osage, gave him nothing but trouble. The new administration in Washington questioned his expenses. He took to drink. On his way east in October 1809, mentally deranged, he shot himself twice, and, it is said, cut himself up with a razor. "I fear O!" wrote Clark. "I fear the waight of his mind has over come him."[13]

William Clark (August 1, 1770–September 1, 1838)

Clark met Meriwether Lewis while both were serving under General "Mad" Anthony Wayne in Ohio in late 1795 and early 1796. Clark was a lieutenant of infantry in the 4th Sub-Legion of the United States Army. Lewis was an ensign (a modern second lieutenant) in the 2nd Sub-Legion. Though Clark outranked Lewis, the two became fast friends; each had the highest respect for the other. Clark resigned from the service in July 1796. Lewis stayed in. They would be reunited on the Ohio River in October 1803.

Both men were Virginians. Clark's family had lived in Albemarle County, home of Lewis and Jefferson, but moved south to Caroline County in 1755. William's parents, John and Ann (Rogers) Clark, had nine children. Their second son, George Rogers Clark, almost 18 years William's senior, was the Virginia hero of the American Revolution, the conqueror of the Illinois country, of Kaskaskia, Cahokia, and Vincennes. William had big shoes to follow. Both boys had red hair.

William Clark grew up without much formal education, but with a solid command of the English language. He was a "turibal" speller. Like another frontiersman, Andrew Jackson, Clark never had much respect for anyone who could think of only one way to spell a word. He outdid himself in his journals with "Sioux," for which he devised 27 ingenious creations, and with "Charbonneau," which he spelled 15 different incorrect ways. Clark knew the ways of the outdoors—riding, hunting, boating, surveying, and natural observations. He was a skilled riverman, a superlative geographer, and a first-rate mapmaker. Most of the sixty maps and charts produced by the Expedition are his. His cumulative map of western America, finished in 1814, remained in service for 50 years. He absorbed the intellectual curiosity of his generation, yet remained "at home in the backwoods," and with backwoodsmen.

Clark's older brothers fought in the American Revolution and one died; brother George became a general. A military career was his by example. His entire family moved to Kentucky in 1785, settling on land staked out by George near Louisville. He inherited the family home Mulberry Hill in 1799, when both his parents died.

Clark's career as a soldier may have begun as early as 1786, when General Clark marched against Indians on the Wabash River. William went on a similar expedition under Col. John Hardin in 1789. In 1791 he was part of General Arthur St. Clair's ill-fated expedition against Miami and Shawnee Indians, although he saw no action. The next year he was a regular army officer.

Clark saw frontier service in Chickasaw territory near Memphis, where the Spanish governor reported that he was "an enterprising youth of extraordinary activity"; at Vincennes, brother George's old stomping ground; and at the pivotal Battle of Fallen Timbers (August 20, 1794), General Wayne's decisive victory over the Miamis, Shawnees, and others on the Maumee River in Ohio. But ill health and family business forced his resignation. He returned to Kentucky to manage George's financial affairs. In one of the great wrongs of American history, the state of Virginia had refused to fully compensate George for his services in its behalf. Beset by creditors, collectors, and demon rum, he needed William's help.

On June 19, 1803, Meriwether Lewis invited Clark to participate with him in the "fatigues," dangers, and honors of the western expedition. "There is no man on earth with whom I should feel equal pleasure in sharing them," he wrote. Clark responded in kind: "My friend, I do assure you that no man lives whith whome I would prefur to undertake Such a Trip."[14] Clark brought complementary skills to the venture, as well as a balanced personality. Even-tempered, friendly, and with a sense of humor, he rarely allowed adverse events to get the better of him. Whereas Meriwether Lewis is described as introverted, melancholic, and moody, Clark is extroverted, even-tempered, and gregarious. He gave the Expedition a steady rudder.

Clark's reward upon return was an appointment as brigadier general of militia in the Louisiana Territory and superintendent of Indian affairs. He moved to St. Louis with his new wife Julia Hancock, who had given her birth name, Judith, to a river in Montana. Clark and Julia had five children; when she died in 1820 he married her cousin Harriet Kennerly and had two more. He named his firstborn Meriwether Lewis

Clark, the surest imaginable sign of enduring friendship. The Clarks also schooled young Jean Baptiste Charbonneau, brought to St. Louis by his father Toussaint in 1810.

Clark held his superintendency for the rest of his active life, until 1838. He held the governorship of Missouri Territory simultaneously, 1813–1821. During the War of 1812 he led a military expedition up the Mississippi River and expelled the British from Prairie du Chien. Afterwards he helped negotiate numerous treaties with Midwestern Indians. An Indian agent in a time of ruthless white expansion was a thankless job. Clark performed superbly. He died peacefully in the home of his son Meriwether.

The Charbonneau Family:
Toussaint Charbonneau (1759?–1843?)
Sacagawea (1788?–1812?)
Jean Baptiste Charbonneau (1805–1866)

The Charbonneaus accompanied Lewis and Clark from Fort Mandan to the Pacific and back, 1805–1806. The parents were employed primarily as interpreters, although each contributed uniquely. Their son, 55 days old at the outset, left no record, but his life became part of the American western experience in the 19th century.

Toussaint Charbonneau, born near Montreal and a veteran of the Canadian fur trade, was living among the Mandan and Hidatsa Indians when Lewis and Clark showed up in 1804. Of French descent, he knew Indian languages and immediately won a job as a translator. In this regard his services on the Expedition were exemplary, especially among the Shoshoni, Flathead, and Nez Perce Indians. Otherwise, he is comic relief. Lewis blamed him for capsizing a pirogue on the Missouri River, when a squall of wind hit the square sail. "Charbono cannot swim and is perhaps the most timid waterman in the world," Lewis explained. Toussaint panicked; only the quick-thinking Pierre Cruzatte, who "threatened to shoot him instantly if he did not take hold of the rudder and do his duty," saved the ship.[15]

Clark once reprimanded Charbonneau "for Strikeng his woman at their Dinner." Lewis called him "a man of no peculiar merit." But in one important respect he earned his keep on the journey. He was a gourmet chef. His specialty was *boudin blanc,* or "white pudding"—sautéed buffalo sausage. It was quite a delicacy.[16]

On Saturday, August 17, 1806, Meriwether Lewis "Settled with Touisant Chabono for his Services as an enterpreter the pric of a horse and Lodge purchased of him for public Service in all amounting to 500 $ 33 1/3 cents."[17] Charbonneau spent the rest of his life on the Missouri, interpreting for a generation of river travelers and fur traders. At age 80 he married a 14-year-old Assiniboine girl. A grizzled old man stares at us from a Karl Bodmer painting of the Mandans in 1834. Is it Toussaint Charbonneau?

Sacagawea is the most famous Indian woman in American history. More statues have been erected to her than to any other American woman. She adorns the new $1 gold coin. Yet we have not the foggiest idea what she looked like, and only a few lines in the journals of Lewis and Clark describe her personality. We do not know when or where she was born, or when, where, or how she died. We are not even sure how to pronounce her name. She is a creation of the American historical imagination, and a brilliant one—an invention, it is said, of the early American feminist movement. She stands for all that American culture demands of a beautiful Indian princess.

She was not the guide or the pilot of the Lewis and Clark Expedition. Lewis and Clark knew as much about the West as she did. She did recognize landmarks as the Expedition approached territory she had known as a child, and she pointed out mountain passes to William Clark. "The indian woman," Clark acknowledged, "has been of great Service to me as a pilot through this Country."[18] She knew roots and berries and edible plants. She inoculated the Expedition against Indian attack—no true war party would include a woman.

Professional historians minimize her accomplishments, but she was more important to the success of the Expedition than her husband, Toussaint Charbonneau. She was a Shoshoni Indian, and the explorers quickly learned that the Shoshoni were the last plains tribe they would encounter before crossing the Rocky Mountains. They needed an entree, a ticket, a guarantee of cordiality. Enter Sacagawea.

November 4, 1804: "a french man by Name Chabonah, who speaks the Big Belley language visit us, he wished to hire & informed us his 2 Squars were Snake Indians, we engau him to go on with us and take one of his wives to interpet the Snake language."[19] Who's more important here? Toussaint could translate Hidatsa into French, but he spoke no Shoshoni. Lewis and Clark hired the man, who took his wife along (violating the rule against married men). He got paid; she did not. But she's the one they needed.

Later that winter Toussaint went on strike, refusing to accompany the Expedition unless he did not have to work or stand guard. Clark was unmoved; he did not beg or plead; he simply let him go. A few days later Charbonneau slunk back into camp and apologized. Did he realize that Clark was taking Sacagawea anyway?

When Charbonneau capsized the pirogue, Sacagawea rescued floating items. "The Indian woman to whom I ascribe equal fortitude and resolution, with any person on board," earned Lewis's compliment.[20]

Sacagawea became deathly ill at the Marias River. Clark "blead" her at least twice, and gave her a "doste of Salts"; she worsened. She complained all night and became "excessively bad"; her case was "somewhat dangerous." Lewis was concerned "from the consideration of her being our only dependence for a friendly negociation with the Snake Indians." He believed "her disorder originated principally from an obstruction of the mensis in consequence of taking could." Clark applied a poultice "exteranely to her region."[21] She might have had gonorrhea. Finally Lewis resorted to the sulphuric waters of a local spring, supplemented by oil of vitriol, saltpeter, and laudanum. Amazingly, Sacagawea recovered.

Sacagawea cinched her legendary status at Camp Fortunate, where she recognized, first, a girlfriend who had also been kidnapped by the Hidatsa but escaped, and next, her long-lost brother, Cameahwait, chief of the Shoshoni. Their meeting was "affecting," and, as planned, it guaranteed safe passage. Sacagawea earned her husband's money. Both Charbonneaus served as interpreters: Cameahwait to Sacagawea in Shoshoni, Sacagawea to Toussaint in Hidatsa, Toussaint to François Labiche in French, and Labiche to Lewis in English. There is no indication, however, that she wanted to drop out and remain with her people.

Sacagawea voted in an election to determine the winter campsite for 1805–1806; she lost. She "was very impotunate to be permited" to see the Pacific; "she had traveled a long way with us to see the great waters"; she won.[22] She returned to the home of her husband without mishap.

Sacagawea was born around 1788, probably on the Lemhi River near modern Tendoy, Idaho. Her name means either "bird woman" or "boat launcher." She died, as best we can tell, in 1812, of "putrid fever," at Fort Manuel on the Missouri River in modern South Dakota.

"[A]bout five oclock this evening one of the wives of Charbono was delivered of a fine boy."[23] Jean Baptiste Charbonneau entered this world on February 11, 1805, with the aid of a potion, administered to his mother, of crushed snake rattles in water. The boy was half Snake Indian, half French. His monument is Pompey's Pillar, or "Pompy's Tower," a massive sandstone bluff on the banks of the Yellowstone River in south-central Montana.

William Clark nicknamed Jean Baptiste "Pomp," or "Pompy," and called him "a butifull promising Child."[24] Clark promised to raise the boy as his own. Sometime in 1809 or 1810 the Charbonneaus delivered their son, now about five, to Clark in St. Louis. Sacagawea's daughter Lisette, born in 1812, became part of Clark's growing family in 1813.

Jean Baptiste spent six years in Europe and Africa (1823–1829) as the protégé of Prince Paul Wilhelm of Württemberg. He learned four languages. Back home, he served as guide and interpreter to a generation of frontiersmen. He lived in California during Gold Rush Days. In 1866, in Oregon on his way to the Montana gold fields, he contracted pneumonia and died. He is buried there, in the southeastern corner of the state, the youngest member of the Corps of Discovery.

York (?–1822?)

York was William Clark's slave, about Clark's age or a few years older, a tall and heavy-set man. He accompanied the Expedition to the Pacific and back, as personal servant, cook, and even hunter. A black man with a gun violated most nineteenth-century stereotypes. York amazed Native Americans with his skin color; the Arikara called him "big medison." He terrified Arikara children with his bluster but was a caring man to Charles Floyd and others. Reports of his sexual prowess are undocumented. He suffered a racial taunt, perhaps, when one of the other men threw sand in his eyes. He voted on the location of winter camp in November 1805, "the first time in American history that a black slave had voted."[25] "York's Islands" in the Missouri River near Townsend, Montana, are his memorial.

Little was known about York's post-Expedition life until the discovery of a cache of Clark's letters in an attic in Louisville, Kentucky, in 1988. We now know that he was married—one of only two married men on the Expedition (the other was John Shields). Indeed, he sent his wife a buffalo robe from Fort Mandan. His wife lived in Louisville. Clark's move to St. Louis with York strained their relationship. At various times Clark threatened to send him to New Orleans and sell him, or to hire him out to a severe master. In 1809 he described York as "insolent and Sulky, I gave him a Severe trouncing."[26] Such was the institution of African slavery.

Sometime after 1816 Clark freed York and set him up in a wagon-freighting business. Apparently, York failed. He probably died of cholera in 1822.

Notes

1. The Declaration of Independence, 4 July 1776, *The Portable Thomas Jefferson*, ed. Merrill D. Peterson, (New York: Viking Press, 1977), 235.

2. Jefferson to Roger C. Weightman, 24 June 1826, *The Portable Thomas Jefferson*, 585.

3. Notes on the State of Virginia, *The Portable Thomas Jefferson*, 217.

4. First Inaugural Address, 4 March 1801, *The Portable Thomas Jefferson*, 292.

5. Notes on the State of Virginia, *The Portable Thomas Jefferson*, 217.

6. *Journals*, V, 7.

7. Quoted in Stephen E. Ambrose, *Undaunted Courage: Meriwether Lewis, Thomas Jefferson, and the Opening of the American West* (New York: Simon & Schuster, 1996), 41, 43.

8. Jefferson to Lewis, 23 February 1801, *Letters of the Lewis and Clark Expedition, with Related Documents, 1783–1854*, ed. Donald Jackson, 2 vols. (Urbana: University of Illinois Press, 1978), I, 2.

9. Quoted in Richard Dillon, *Meriwether Lewis: A Biography* (New York: Coward-McCann, 1965), 15.

10. Jefferson to Paul Allen, 18 August 1813, *Letters*, II, 589–90.

11. Levi Lincoln to Jefferson, 17 April 1803; Jefferson's Instructions to Lewis, 20 June 1803, *Letters*, I, 35, 64.

12. Jefferson to Paul Allen, 18 August 1813, *Letters*, II, 591–92.

13. Clark to Jonathan Clark, 28 October 1809, *Dear Brother: Letters of William Clark to Jonathan Clark*, ed. James J. Holmberg (New Haven, Conn.: Yale University Press, 2002), 218.

14. Lewis to Clark, 19 June 1803; Clark to Lewis, 18 July 1803, *Letters*, I, 60, 110–11.

15. *Journals*, IV, 152–53, May 14, 1805. The best brief introduction to Toussaint, Sacagawea, and Jean Baptiste is Irving W. Anderson, "A Charbon-

neau Family Portrait: Profiles of the American West," *American West* 17, 2 (1980): 4–13, 58–64.

16. *Journals,* V, 93, August 14, 1805; Jackson, ed., *Letters,* I, 369; *Journals,* IV, 131.

17. *Journals,* VIII, 305.

18. *Journals,* VIII, 180.

19. *Journals,* III, 228.

20. *Journals,* IV, 157.

21. *Journals,* IV, 277, 279, 287, 294, 297, 299, 301.

22. *Journals,* VI, 168.

23. *Journals,* III, 291.

24. *Journals,* VIII, 305.

25. Ambrose, *Undaunted Courage,* 311.

26. Holmberg, ed., *Dear Brother,* 201.

PRIMARY DOCUMENTS OF THE LEWIS AND CLARK EXPEDITION

Document 1
Jefferson's Instructions to Lewis, June 20, 1803

To Captain Meriwether Lewis esq. Capt. Of the 1st regimt. of Infantry of the U.S. of A.

Your situation as Secretary of the President of the U.S. has made you acquainted with the objects of my confidential message of Jan. 18, 1803 to the legislature; you have seen the act they passed, which, tho' expressed in general terms, was meant to sanction those objects, and you are appointed to carry them into execution.

Instruments for ascertaining, by celestial observations, the geography of the country through which you will pass, have been already provided. Light articles for barter and presents among the Indians, arms for your attendants, say for from 10. to 12. men, boats, tents, & other travelling apparatus, with ammunition, medecine, surgical instruments and provisions you will have prepared with such aids as the Secretary at War can yield in his department; & from him also you will receive authority to engage among our troops, by voluntary agreement, the number of attendants above mentioned, over whom you, as their commanding officer, are invested with all the powers the laws give in such a case.

As your movements while within the limits of the U.S. will be better directed by occasional communications, adapted to circumstances as they arise, they will not be noticed here. What follows will respect your proceedings after your departure from the United states.

Your mission has been communicated to the ministers here from France, Spain & Great Britain, and through them to their governments; & such assurances given them as to it's objects, as we trust will satisfy them. The country *<of Louisiana>* having been ceded by Spain to France, *<and possession by this time probably given,>* the passport you have from the minister of France, the representative of the present sovereign of the country, will be a protection with all it's subjects; & that from the minister of England will entitle you to the friendly aid of any traders of that allegiance with whom you may happen to meet.

The object of your mission is to explore the Missouri river, & such principal stream of it, as, by it's course and communication with the waters of the Pacific ocean, whether the Columbia, Oregan, Colorado or any other river may offer the most direct & practicable water communication across this continent for the purposes of commerce.

Beginning at the mouth of the Missouri, you will take *<careful>* observations of latitude & longitude, at all remarkeable points on the river, & especially at the mouths of rivers, at rapids, at islands, & other places & objects distinguished by such natural marks & characters of a durable kind, as that they may with certainty be recognised hereafter. The courses of the river between these points of observation may be supplied by the compass the log-line & by time, corrected by the observations themselves. The variations of the compass too, in different places, should be noticed.

The interesting points of the portage between the heads of the Missouri, & of the water offering the best communication with the Pacific ocean, should also be fixed by observation, & the course of the water to the ocean, in the same manner as that of the Missouri.

Your observations are to be taken with great pains & accuracy, to be entered distinctly & intelligibly for others as well as yourself, to comprehend all the elements necessary, with the aid of the usual tables, to fix the latitude and longitude of the places at which they were taken, and are to be rendered to the war-office, for the purpose of having the calculations made concurrently by proper persons within the U.S. Several copies of these as well as of your other notes should be made at leisure times, & put into the care of the most trust-worthy of your attendants, to guard, by multiplying them, against the accidental losses to which they will be exposed. A further guard would be that one of these copies be on the paper of the birch, as less liable to injury from damp than common paper.

The commerce which may be carried on with the people inhabiting the line you will pursue, renders a knolege of those people important. You will therefore endeavor to make yourself acquainted, as far as a diligent pursuit of your journey shall admit, with the names of the nations & their numbers;

the extent & limits of their possessions;
their relations with other tribes of nations;
their language, traditions, monuments;
their ordinary occupations in agriculture, fishing, hunting, war, arts & the
    implements for these;
their food, clothing, & domestic accomodations;
the diseases prevalent among them, & the remedies they use;
moral & physical circumstances which distinguish them from the tribes we
    know;
peculiarities in their laws, customs & dispositions;
and articles of commerce they may need or furnish, & to what extent.

And, considering the interest which every nation has in extending & strengthening the authority of reason & justice among the people around them, it will be useful to acquire what knolege you can of the state of morality, religion, & information among them; as it may better enable those who may endeavor to civilize & instruct them, to adapt their measures to the existing notions & practices of those on whom they are to operate.

Other objects worthy of notice will be the soil & face of the country, it's growth
    & vegetable productions, especially those not of the U.S.
the animals of the country generally, & especially those not known in the U.S.
the remains or accounts of any which may be deemed rare or extinct;
the mineral productions of every kind; but more particularly metals, lime-
    stone, pit coal, & saltpetre; salines & mineral waters, noting the tempera-
    ture of the last, & such circumstances as may indicate their character;
volcanic appearances;
climate, as characterised by the thermometer, by the proportion of rainy, cloudy,
    & clear days, by lightning, hail, snow, ice, by the access & recess of frost, by
    the winds prevailing at different seasons, the dates at which particular plants

put forth or lose their flower, or leaf, times of appearance of particular birds, reptiles or insects.

Altho' your route will be along the channel of the Missouri, yet you will endeavor to inform yourself, by enquiry, of the character & extent of the country watered by it's branches, & especially on it's Southern side. The North river or Rio Bravo which runs into the gulph of Mexico, and the North river, or Rio colorado which runs into the gulph of California, are understood to be the principal streams heading opposite to the waters of the Missouri, and running Southwardly. Whether the dividing grounds between the Missouri & them are mountains or flat lands, what are their distance from the Missouri, the character of the intermediate country, & the people inhabiting it, are worthy of particular enquiry. The Northern waters of the Missouri are less to be enquired after, because they have been ascertained to a considerable degree, & are still in a course of ascertainment by English traders, and travellers. But if you can learn any thing certain of the most Northern source of the Missisipi, & of it's position relatively to the lake of the woods, it will be interesting to us.

<*Two copies of your notes at least & as many more as leisure will admit, should be made & confided to the care of the most trusty individuals of your attendants.*> Some account too of the path of the Canadian traders from the Missisipi, at the mouth of the Ouisconsing to where it strikes the Missouri, & of the soil and rivers in it's course, is desireable.

In all your intercourse with the natives, treat them in the most friendly & conciliatory manner which their own conduct will admit; allay all jealousies as to the object of your journey, satisfy them of it's innocence, make them acquainted with the position, extent, character, peaceable & commercial dispositions of the U.S. [,] of our wish to be neighborly, friendly & useful to them, & of our dispositions to a commercial intercourse with them; confer with them on the points most convenient as mutual emporiums, and the articles of most desireable interchange for them & us. If a few of their influential chiefs, within practicable distance, wish to visit us, arrange such a visit with them, and furnish them with authority to call on our officers, on their entering the U.S. to have them conveyed to this place at the public expence. If any of them should wish to have some of their young people brought up with us, & taught such arts as may be useful to them, we will receive, instruct & take care of them. Such a mission, whether of influential chiefs or of young people, would give some security to your own party. Carry with you some matter of the kinepox; inform those of them with whom you may be, of it's efficacy as a preservative from the smallpox; & instruct & encourage them in the use of it. This may be especially done wherever you winter.

As it is impossible for us to foresee in what manner you will be received by those people, whether with hospitality or hostility, so is it impossible to prescribe the exact degree of perseverance with which you are to pursue your journey. We value too much the lives of citizens to offer them to probable destruction. Your numbers will be sufficient to secure you against the unauthorised opposition of individuals or of small parties: but if a superior force, authorised, or not authorised, by a nation, should be arrayed against your further passage, and inflexibly determined to arrest it, you must decline it's farther pursuit, and return. In the loss of yourselves, we should lose also the information you will have acquired. By returning safely with that, you may enable us to renew the essay with better calculated means. To your own discretion therefore must be left the degree of danger you may risk, and the point at which you should decline, only saying we wish you to err on the side of your safety, and to bring back your party safe even if it be with less information.

As far up the Missouri as the white settlements extend, an intercourse will probably be found to exist between them & the Spanish posts of St. Louis opposite Cahokia, or Ste. Genevieve opposite Kaskaskia. From still further up the river, the traders may furnish a conveyance for letters. Beyond that, you may perhaps be able to engage Indians to bring letters for the government to Cahokia or Kaskaskia, on promising that they shall there receive such special compensation as you shall have stipulated with them. Avail yourself of these means to communicate to us, at seasonable intervals, a copy of your journal, notes & observations, of every kind, putting into cypher whatever might do injury if betrayed.

Should you reach the Pacific ocean inform yourself of the circumstances which may decide whether the furs of those parts may not be collected as advantageously at the head of the Missouri (convenient as is supposed to the waters of the Colorado & Oregon or Columbia) as at Nootka sound, or any other point of that coast; and that trade be consequently conducted through the Missouri & U.S. more beneficially than by the circumnavigation now practised.

On your arrival on that coast endeavor to learn if there be any port within your reach frequented by the sea-vessels of any nation, & to send two of your trusty people back by sea, in such a way as <*they shall judge*> shall appear practicable, with a copy of your notes: and should you be of opinion that the return of your party by the way they went will be eminently dangerous, then ship the whole, & return by sea, by the way either of cape Horn, or the cape of good Hope, as you shall be able. As you will be without money, clothes or provisions, you must endeavor to use the credit of the U.S. to obtain them, for which purpose open letters of credit shall be furnished you, authorising you to draw upon the Executive of the U.S. or any of it's officers, in any part of the world, on which draughts can be disposed of, & to apply with our recommendations to the Consuls, agents, merchants, or citizens of any nation with which we have intercourse, assuring them, in our name, that any aids they may furnish you, shall be honorably repaid, and on demand. Our consuls Thomas Hewes at Batavia in Java, Wm. Buchanan in the Isles of France & Bourbon & John Elmslie at the Cape of good Hope will be able to supply your necessities by draughts on us.

Should you find it safe to return by the way you go, after sending two of your party round by sea, or with your whole party, if no conveyance by sea can be found, do so; making such observations on your return, as may serve to supply, correct or confirm those made on your outward journey.

On re-entering the U.S. and reaching a place of safety, discharge any of your attendants who may desire & deserve it, procuring for them immediate paiment of all arrears of pay & cloathing which may have incurred since their departure, and assure them that they shall be recommended to the liberality of the legislature for the grant of a souldier's portion of land each, as proposed in my message to Congress: & repair yourself with your papers to the seat of government <*to which I have only to add my sincere prayer for your safe return*>.

To provide, on the accident of your death, against anarchy, dispersion, & the consequent danger to your party, and total failure of the enterprize, you are hereby authorised, by any instrument signed & written in your own hand, to name the person among them who shall succeed to the command on your decease, and by like instruments to change the nomination from time to time as further experience of the characters accompanying you shall point out superior fitness: and all the powers and authorities given to yourself are, in the event of your death, transferred to, & vested in the successor so named, with further power to him, and his successors in like manner to name each his successor, who, on the death of his predecessor, shall be invested with all the powers & authorities given to yourself.

Given under my hand at the city of Washington this 20th day of June 1803.

TH: J. Pr. U.S. of A.

Source: Jefferson's Instructions to Lewis, June 20, 1803, in Donald Jackson, ed., *Letters of the Lewis and Clark Expedition, with Related Documents, 1783–1854,* 2nd ed., 2 vols. (Urbana: University of Illinois Press, 1978), I, 61–66.

Document 2
Lewis & Clark to the Oto Indians, August 4, 1804

To the Petit Voleur, or Wear-ruge-nor, the great Chief of the Ottoes, to the Chiefs and Warriors of the Ottoes, and the Chiefs and Warriors of the Missouri nation residing with the Ottoes–

Children. Convene from among you the old men of experience; the men, on the wisdom of whose judgement you are willing to risk the future happiness of your nations; and the warriors, to the strength of whose arms you have been taught to look for protection in the days of danger. When in Council tranquilly assembled, reflect on the time past, and that to come; do not deceive yourselves, nor suffer others to deceive you; but like men and warriors devoted to the real interests of their nation, seek those truths; which can alone perpetuate its happiness.

Children. Commissioned and sent by the great Chief of the Seventeen great nations of America, we have come to inform you, as we go also to inform all the nations of red men who inhabit the borders of the Missouri, that a great council was lately held between this great chief of the Seventeen great nations of America, and your old fathers the french and Spaniards; and that in this great council it was agreed that all the white men of Louisiana, inhabiting the waters of the Missouri and Mississippi should obey the commands of this great chief; he has accordingly adopted them as his children and they now form one common family with us: your old traders are of this description; they are no longer the subjects of France or Spain, but have become the Citizens of the Seventeen great nations of america, and are bound to obey the commands of their great Chief the President who is now your only great father.

Children. This council being concluded between your old fathers the french and Spaniards, and your great father the Chief of the Seventeen great nations of America, your old fathers the French and Spaniards in complyance with their engagements made in that council, have withdrawn all their troops from all their military posts on the waters of the Mississippi and missouri, and have Surrendered to our great cheif all their fortifications and lands in this country, together with the mouths of all the rivers through which the traders bring goods to the red men on the troubled waters. These arangements being made, your old fathers the french and Spaniards have gone beyond the great lake towards the rising Sun, from whence they never intend returning to visit their former red-children in this quarter; nor will they, or any other nation of white men, ever again display their flag on the troubled waters; because the mouths of all those rivers are in the possession of the great Chief of the Seventeen great nations of America, who will command his war chiefs to suffer no vessel to pass–but those which sail under the protection of his flag, and who acknowledge his Supreme authority.

Children. From what has been said, you will readily perceive, that the great chief of the Seventeen great nations of America, has become your only father; he is the only father; he is the only friend to whom you can now look for protection, or from whom you can ask favours, or receive good councils, and he will take care that you shall have no just cause to regret this change; he will serve you, & not deceive you.

Children. The great chief of the Seventeen great nations of America, impelled by his parental regard for his newly adopted children on the troubled waters, has sent us out to clear the road, remove every obstruction, and to make it the road of peace between himself and his red children residing there; to enquire into the Nature of their wants, and on our return to inform Him of them, in order that he may make the necessary arrangements for their relief, he has sent by us, one of his flags, a medal and some cloathes, such as he dresses his war chiefs with, which he directed should be given to the great chief of the Ottoe nation, to be kept by him, as a pledge of the sincerity with which he now offers you the hand of friendship.

Children. Know that the great chief who has thus offered you the hand of unalterable friendship, is the great Chief of the Seventeen great Nations of America, whose cities are as numerous as the stars of the heavens, and whose people like the grass of your plains, cover with their Cultivated fields and wigwams, the wide Extended country, reaching from the western borders of the Mississippi, to the great lakes of the East, where the land ends and the Sun rises from the face of the great waters.

Children. Know that this great chief, as powerfull as he is just, and as beneficient as he is wise, always entertaining a sincere and friendly disposition towards the red people of America, has commanded us his war chiefs to undertake this long journey, which we have so far accomplished with great labour & much expence, in order to council with yourselves and his other red-children on the troubled waters, to give you his good advice; to point out to you the road in which you must walk to obtain happiness. He has further commanded us to tell you that when you accept his flag and medal, you accept therewith his hand of friendship, which will never be withdrawn from your nation as long as you continue to follow the councils which he may command his chiefs to give you, and shut your ears to the councils of Bad birds.

Children. The road in which your great father and friend, has commanded us to tell you and your nation that you must walk in order to enjoy the benefit of his friendship, is, that you are to live in peace with all the *white men,* for they are his children; neither wage war against the *red men* your neighbours, for they are equally his children and he is bound to protect them. Injure not the persons of any traders who may come among you, neither destroy nor take their property from them by force; more particularly those traders who visit you under the protection of your great fathers flag. Do not obstruct the passage of any boat, pirogue, or other vessel, which may be ascending or decending the Missouri River, more especially such as may be under cover of your great fathers flag neither injure any red or white man on board such vessels as may possess the flag, for by that signal you may know them to be good men, and that they do not intend to injure you; they are therefore to be treated as friends, and as the common children of one great father, (the great chief of the Seventeen great nations of America.

Children. Do these things which your great father advises and be happy. Avoid the councils of bad birds; turn on your heel from them as you would from the precipice of a high rock, whose summit reached the Clouds, and whose base was washed by the gulph of human woes; lest by one false step you should bring upon your nation the displeasure of your great father, the great chief of the Seventeen great nations of America, who could consume you as the fire consumes the grass of the plains. The mouths of all the rivers through which the traders bring goods to you are in his possession, and if you displease him he could at pleasure shut them up and prevent his traders from coming among you; and this would of course bring all the Calamities of want upon you; but it is not the wish of your great father to injure you, on the contrary he is now pursuing the measures best Calculated to insure your happiness.

Children. If you open your ears to the councils of your great father, the great chief of the Seventeen great nations of America, & strictly pursue the advice which he has now given you through us, he will as soon as possible after our return, send a store of goods to the mouth of the river Platte to trade with you for pelteries and furs; these goods will be furnished you annually in a regular manner, and in such quantities as will be equal to all your necessities. You will then obtain goods on much better terms than you have ever received them heretofore.

Children. As it will necessarily take some time before we can return, and your great father send and establish this store of goods; he will permit your old traders who reside among you, or who annually visit you, to continue to trade with you, provided they give you good Council.

Children. We are now on a long journey to the head of the Missouri; the length of this journey compelled us to load our boat and perogues with provisions, we have therefore brought very few goods as presents for yourselves or any other nations which we may meet on our way. We are no traders, but have come to consult you on the subject of your trade; to open the road and prepare the way, in order that your nation may hereafter receive a regular and plentifull supply of goods.

Children. We are sorry that your absence from your town prevented our seeing your great chief and yourselves; it would have given us much pleasure to have spoken to you personnally; but as the cold season is fast advancing, and we have a long distance to travel, we could not wait for your return.

Children. If your great Chief wishes to see your great father and speak with him, he can readily do so. Let your chief engage some trader who may reside with you the ensuing winter, to take him and four of his principal chiefs or warriors with him to St. Louis when he returns thither on the ensuing spring; your great chief may take with him also an interpreter of his own choice, who shall be well paid for his services by your great father's Chiefs; the trader will also be well paid for his services by the Commandant at St. Louis. The commandant at St. Louis will furnish you with the necessary number of horses, and all other means to make your journey from thence to your great father's town Comfortable and safe.

Children. In order that the Commandant at St. Louis, as well as your great father, and all his chiefs may know you, you must take with you, the flag, the medal and this parole which we now send you. When your great father and his chiefs see those things, they will know that you have opened your ears to your great father's voice, and have come to hear his good Councils.

Our oldest son the Wear-ruge-nor. If the situation of your nation is such that you cannot with propriety leave them, you may send some of your principal men not exceeding five, to see your great father and hear his words. You must give them authority to act for you and your Nation. Your great father will receive them as his children, give them his good councils, and send them back loaded with presents for their nation; your nation would then see that all we have told you is true, and that the great chief of the Seventeen great nations of America never sends his red children from him to return with empty hands to their village.

Our oldest son the Wear-ruge-nor. Whomsoever you send to your great father must carry the flag and this parole, in order that your great father and his chiefs may know that they have come to see them by our invitation. Send by them also all the flags and medals which you may have received from your old fathers the French and Spaniards, or from any other nation whatever, your father will give you new flags and new medals of his own in exchange for those which you send him. It is not proper since you have become the children of the great chief of the Seventeen great nations of America, that you should wear or keep those emblems of attachment to any other great father but himself, nor will it be pleasing to him if you continue to do so.

Children. We hope that the great Spirit will open your ears to our councils, and dispose your minds to their observance. Follow these councils and you will have nothing to fear, because the great Spirit will smile upon your nation, and in future ages will make you to outnumber the trees of the forest.

Signed and sealed this 4th day of August 1804 at the council Bluff, by us, the friends of all the red-men, and the war chiefs of the great chief of the Seventeen great nations of America.

> MERIWETHER LEWIS CAPTN.
> 1st U.S. Regt. Infantry.
> WILLIAM CLARK
> Capt. On the Missouri Expedition

Source: Lewis and Clark to the Oto Indians, August 4, 1804, in Donald Jackson, ed., *Letters of the Lewis and Clark Expedition, with Related Documents, 1783–1854,* 2nd ed., 2 vols. (Urbana: Univeersity of Illinois Press, 1978), I, 203–8.

Document 3
François-Antoine Larocque's "Missouri Journal," 1804–1805

Saturday 24th [November, 1804]. Sett off at sun rise, 2 hours after met with two of the Big Belly [Hidatsa] Indians, who were going a hunting, they appeared to be well pleased to see us. Smoked a pipe with them & proceeded. At mid day Saw the smoke of one of the big B. Villages, to the South of which we passed, at 2 arrived at another of their villages, where I Enquired for Charbonneax (it being his usual place of Residence) & was Informed by an HB [Hudson's Bay] man who is there for the purpose of trade, that he was with some Americans, below the Mandan villages to whom he was Engaged. Being unwilling to leave the HB here alone to get the whole trade of this village, I got the Horses unloaded & made a small Equipt. of goods, which I gave in Charge to Mr. McKenzie.

Sunday 25th. Left Morrison with Mr. McK. in the best Lodge we Could find & proceeded to the Mandan villages, with the Remainder of the goods (Excepting an Equipt. destined for the upper villages of the B. Bellys). On the Road thither, met with Captain Lewis, Chief of the American party (with Jusseaum & Charbonneaux), had about a quarter of an hour Conversation with him, during which he Invited me to his house & appeared very friendly.

Arrived at the Mandan village at 3 P.M. Entered in the Lodge of the Black Cat the Chief of that village. Sent for the Grand, the Chief of the other Mandan village. Gave them both a Chiefs Cloathing, & Explained to them the motive of my coming &c &c. Gave a pipe of Tob. to all the grown men as usual. Sent Azure & McKay, with the Grand, on the other side of the River, with an Equipt. of goods in Charge of Azure.

Monday 26th. Lafrance traded 350 skins in wolves [and] in kitts, from the Indians of this village, he being the person, to whom I gave this outfit in Charge. The Indians appeared to be of a very thievish disposition.

Tuesday 27th. Went over to see Azure & what trade he had which was about 250 plues. Returned to the Blk. Cats. Cap't Lewis Return'd from above & stopp'd at the Lodge. Spoke to Charbonneau about helping, as Interpreter in the trade to the big Bellies, he told me that being Engaged to the Americans, he Could not Come without leave from Capt. Lewis & desired me to speak to him—which I did. Capt Lewis told me that as he had no business for Charbonneau, but at times during the winter, he had no objection to his helping me, upon Certain Conditions, which agreeing to, Charbonneau promised me, that he would Come next morning.

Wednesday 28th. The Blk. Cat went to dine with the Americans, with 2 other Chiefs upon an Invitation from Capt. Lewis, who had also Invited me, but expecting Charbonneau, I declined going. Exceeding bad weather, wind N.E. & snowing very hard.

Thursday 29th. Still very bad weather which as I thought prevented Charbonneaux from Coming. In the Evening the weather cleared, went to see what was the Reason he did not come, was very politely Received, by Capts. Lewis & Clarke & pass'd the night with them. Just as I arrived, they were dispatching a man for me, having heard that I Intended giving Flags & medals to the Indians which they forbid me from giving in the name of the United States, saying that Government, look'd upon those things, as the Sacred Emblem of the attachment of the Indians to their Country. But as I had neither Flags, nor medals, I Ran no Risk of disobeying those orders, of which I assured them.

They next Called Charbonneau, & gave him leave to Come with me, but strictly enjoined him not to utter a word, which might any way be to the prejudice of the United States or of any of its Citizens, to the

Indians, although I should order him to so to do, which (say they), turning to me, we are very far from thinking you would.

Their party Consists of 40 odd men besides themselves, & are sent by Government for the purpose of Exploring the N.W. Countries, to the Pacific Ocean so as to settle the Boundary Line between, the British & the American territories. Likewise to make it known to the Indians, on the Missouri, & the adjacent Countries that they are under, the Government of the big Knives, who will protect them & supply them with all their wants, as long as they shall behave as dutifull Children to their Great Father the President of the United States &c (which has been the Continued subject of their Harangues to the Indians, throughout the Winter).

They showed me their passports & Letters of Recommendation from the french, Spanish & British Ministers at the City of Washington, which say the object of their voyage is purely scientific & Literary, & no ways Concerning, trade, desiring all persons under their Respective Governments, to aid & assist, that party as much as in their power lies, in Case they should be in want of any thing in the Course of their Voyage. They have likewise Letters of Credit from the American Government for the payment of any draughts, they should draw upon it.

They left Philadelphia in the spring 1803. Came down the Ohio & pass'd the winter at the mouth of the Missouri at St. Lewis in the Illinois Country. It took them the whole summer to Come to the Mandans, at which place they arrived in October last. They made treaties of peace with all the Indian Nations they saw on their Road, excepting the Sioux's, with whom they were very near Coming to an Engagement. They made presents of a Flag, Medal, Chiefs Cloathing, tobacco, knives, Beads & other trinkets, to Every Chief of the Indian nations, which they saw, but have not given a single shot of amunition.

They told me that it was not the policy of the United States to Restrain Commerce & fetter it, as was the Case when Louisiana belonged to the Spanish, that we & all persons who should Come on their territories, for trade or for any other purpose, will never be molested by an American Officer or Commandant, unless his behaviour was such as would subject an American Citizen himself to punishment. Nor will any trader be obliged to pay for permission to trade, as was formerly the Case under the Spanish, as no Exclusive privilege will be granted. Every one shall be free to trade after his own manner. One thing that Government may do, as it has already done, about Detroit & other places, where opposition in trade Ran high, is to have a public store, well assorted of all kind of Indian goods, which store, is to be open'd to the Indians, only when the traders, in opposition Run to too Excessive lengths; for the purpose of under selling them, & by that means, keep them quiet. No Derouines to take place, no Liquor to be sold (that is, of a Spirituous kinds) &c &c. In short, during the time I was there, a very Grand Plan was schemed, but its taking place is more than I can tell although the Captains say they are well assured it will.

Friday 30th. Returned to the Mandans. Charbonneau got Ready to Come with me, but just as he Was setting off, he Received orders to follow Capt. Clarke who was going, with 25 men, to join a party of Mandans, & Repulse a some Siouxs, who kill'd a Mandan yesterday & were supposed to be in the neighbourhood. Went to see Azure, & give him directions how to make the packs as I intend to send to the Fort very soon, having wherewith to load the Co/ horses.

Friday 18th [January 1805]. Went down to Fort Mandan, in the morning, to Return a book I had borrow'd, & to see if there was any particular news. Arrived there at 3 P.M. & Remain'd the whole day.

Sunday, 20th. Captain Clarke upon being Informed that I had to take Care of the horses myself, & that they were in danger of being thieved, desired I would send them down, & that he would have them taken Care of with his own.

My Landlord went down to the Americans to get his Gun Mended. They have a very Expert smith, who is always Employed in making dift. things & working for the Indians, who are grown very fond of them although they disliked them at first.

Source: François-Antoine Larocque's "Missouri Journal," Winter, 1804–1805, in W. Raymond Wood and Thomas D. Thiessen, eds., *Early Fur Trade on the Northern Plains: Canadian Traders among the Mandan and Hidatsa Indians,1738–1818* (Norman: University of Oklahoma Press, 1985), 136–40, 149–50.

Document 4
Charles McKenzie's "First Expedition to the Mississouri, 1804"

Here we also found a party of forty Americans under the command of Captains Lewis and Clark exploring a passage by the Mississouri to the Pacific Ocean– they came up the River in a Boat of twenty oars accompanied by two *Peroques*. Their fortifications for winter Quarters were already complete– they had held a council with the Mandanes, and distributed many presents; but most of the Chiefs did not accept any thing from them. Some time after Captain Lewis with three Inter-preters paid a visit to the *Gros Ventres* Village, and went directly to the Serpents Lodge where he passed the night; next morning he came to the village where I was– and observed to me that he was not very graciously received at the upper Village. "I sent a word, said he, to inform *Le Blet qui porte les cornes* ["The large one who wears horns"] that I intended to take up my Quarters at his Lodge– he returned for answer that he was not a[t] home; this conduct surprised me, it being common only among your English Lords not to be at home, when they did not wish to see strangers. But as I had felt no inclination of entering any house after being told the Landlord would not be at home, I looked out for another lodging which I readily found."

After haranguing the Indians and explaining to them the purport of his expedition to the Westward, several of them accepted clothing– but notwithstanding they could not be reconciled to *like* the strangers as they called them:– "Had these Whites come amongst us, Said the Chiefs, with charitable views they would have loaded their Great Boat with necessaries. It is true they have ammunition but they prefer throw-ing it away idly than sparing a shot of it to a poor Mandane." The Indi-ans admired the air Gun as it could discharge forty shots out of one load– but they dreaded the magic of the owners. "Had I these White warriors in the upper plains, said the *Gros Ventres*, Chief, my young men on horseback would soon do for them, as they would do for so many wolves– for, continued he, there are only two sensible men among them– the worker of Iron, and the mender of Guns."

Mr. La Roque and I having nothing very particular claiming atten-tion, we lived contentedly and became intimate with the Gentlemen of the American expedition; who on all occasions seemed happy to see us, and always treated us with civility and kindness. It is true Captain Lewis could not make himself agreeable to us–he could speak fluently and learnedly on all subjects, but his inveterate disposition against the British stained, at least in our eyes, all his eloquence. Captain Clark was equally well informed, but his conversation was always pleasant, for he seemed to dislike giving offence unnecessarily.–

The Missouri was free of ice the Second of April. Then the American Gentlemen sent off their twenty oar Boat with ten men for the United States; and on the 8th. following the Expedition proceeded up the River towards the Rocky Mountains. It consisted of one large peroque; and seven small wooden Canoes–containing the commanding officers, thirty men, and a woman–the woman who answered the purpose of wife to Charbonneau was of the Serpent Nation, and lately taken prisoner by a war party:–She understood a little Gros Ventre, in which she had to converse with her husband, who was a Canadian, and who did not understand English–A Mulatto who spoke bad French and worse English served as Interpreter to the Captains– So that a single word to be understood by the party required to pass from the Natives to the woman, from the woman to the husband, from the husband to the Mulatto, from the Mulatto to the Captain. I was once present when vocabularies were making of the languages of the Mandane Villages. The two Frenchmen who happened to be the medium of information had warm disputes upon the meaning of every word that was taken down by the expedition– as the Indians could not well comprehend the intention of recording their words, they concluded that the Americans had a wicked design upon their Country.–

Source: Charles McKenzie, First Expedition to the Mississouri, in W. Raymond Wood and Thomas D. Thiessen, eds., *Early Fur Trade on the Northern Plains: Canadian Traders among the Mandan and Hidatsa Indians,1738–1818* (Norman: University of Oklahoma Press, 1985), 232–33, 238–39.

Document 5A
Nicholas Biddle

Saturnalia Bisontina

January 5th. We had high and boisterous winds last night and this morning. The Indians continue to purchase repairs with grain of different kinds. In the first village there has been a buffalo-dance for the last three nights, which has put them all into commotion, and the description which we received from those of the party who visited the village, and from other sources, is not a little ludicrous.

The buffalo-dance is an institution originally intended for the benefit of the old men, and practiced at their suggestion. When buffalo become scarce they send a man to harangue the village, declaring that the game is far off and that a feast is necessary to bring it back; if the village be disposed a day and place is named for the celebration. At the appointed hour the old men arrive and seat themselves cross-legged on skins, round a fire in the middle of the lodge, with a sort of doll or small image, dressed like a female, placed before them. The young men bring them a platter of provisions, a pipe of tobacco, and their wives, whose dress on the occasion is only a robe or mantle loosely thrown around the body. On their arrival each youth selects the old man he means to distinguish by his favor, and spreads before him the provisions, after which he presents the pipe and smokes with him.

Mox senex vir simulacrum parvae puellae ostensit. Tunc egrediens coetu, jecit effigium solo et superincumbens, senili ardore veneris complexit. Hoc est signum. Denique uxor e turba recessit, et jactu corporis, fovet amplexus viri solo recubante. Maritus appropinquans senex vir dejecto vultu, et honorem et dignitatem ejus conservare amplexu uxoris illum oravit. Forsitan imprimis ille refellit; dehinc, maritus multis precibus, multis lacrymis, et multis donis vehementer intercessit. Tunc senex amator perculsus misericordia, tot precibus, tot lacrymis, et tot donis, conjugali amplexu submisit. Multum ille jactatus est, sed debilis et effoetus senectute, frustra jactatus est. Maritus interdum, stans juxta, gaudet multum honore, et ejus dignitate sic conservata. Unus nostrum sodalium, multum alacrior et potentior juventute, hac nocte honorem quatuor maritorum custodivit.

Source: [Nicholas Biddle] *History of the Expedition under the Command of Lewis and Clark,* Elliott Coues, ed., 3 vols. (1893; reprint, New York: Dover, 1965), I, 221–22.

Document 5B
Biddle's Notes

5th Jany. 1805. Buff[alo]e Dance–a dance for the benefit of the old men. They, about the time buffe. is scarce, appoint a man to harangue village saying buffe. is far off & they must have a feast to bring them back–name a certain night & place for it. The young married men prepare provisions (a platter) pipe & tobacco which they take to the feast–their wives accompy. them with nothing on except a robe or mantle round them–feast in a house–the old men assemble first seat thems[elves] in a ring on skins cross legged around a fire in the middle of the house. They have before them a sort of small doll dressed like a woman–when the young men & their [wives] arrive the young man chooses the old one whom he means to favor–& to whom he gives the provisions–the old men eat–after which the young man gives the old man a lighted pipe & smokes with him–the [young man] then asks the old man in a whining tone to do him honor by indulging himself with his wife which he brings up to him–the old man follows the woman out of the door. After smoking a particular o.m. appointed for the purpose takes the image in his arms carries her out of doors lies down on it with appearance of copulation. This is the signal for the young men who are in the rear of the circle with their wives behind them to lead them up to o.m. naked except the robe. The woman arrived out of doors unfolds her robe lies down & invites & receives his embraces. Sometimes the o.m. can scarcely walk. If the old man wants to get a present from husband goes only to the door–the wife informs the husband who sends for a robe & some articles of dress & throws at the feet of the old man & begs that he will not despise or disgrace him, but return to his wife. If present insufficient still lingers till increased by husband. If he receives it he is bound to go. The o.m. if he cannot do the substantial service must go thro' the forms which saves the honor of the parties. This ceremony over–the o.m. smoke together & the y.m. dance together. Indian women do not dance together ever. White men are always considered as o.m. & are generally preferred by the Squaws because they will give probably some present and for other obvious reasons.

Source: The Nicholas Biddle Notes, c. April 1810, in Donald Jackson, ed., *Letters of the Lewis and Clark Expedition, with Related Documents, 1783–1854*, 2nd ed., 2 vols. (Urbana: University of Illinois Press, 1978), II, 538.

Document 5C
William Clark

5th of January Satturday 1805

    a cold day Some Snow, Several Indians visit us with thier axes to get them mended, I imploy my Self drawing a Connection of the Countrey from what information I have recved–a Buffalow Dance (or Medison) for 3 nights passed in the 1st Village, a curious Custom the old men arrange themselves in a circle & after Smoke a pipe, which is handed them by a young man, Dress up for the purpose, the young men who have their wives back of the circle go to one of the old men with a whining tone and [*request?*] the old man to take his wife (who presents necked except a robe) and–(or Sleep with him) the Girl then takes the Old man (who verry often can Scercely walk) and leades him to a Convenient place for the business, after which they return to the lodge, if the Old man (or a white man) returns to the lodge without gratifying the man & his wife, he offers her again and again; it is often the Case that after the 2d time <he> without Kissing the Husband throws a nice robe over the old man & begs him not to dispise him, & his wife

(we Sent a man to this Medisan <Dance> last night, they gave him 4 Girls) all this is to cause the buffalow to Come near So that They may kill thim

Source: William Clark, Saturday, January 5, 1805, in Gary E. Moulton, ed., *The Journals of the Lewis and Clark Expedition,* 13 vols. (Lincoln: University of Nebraska Press, 1983–2001), III, 268.

Document 5D
Walter Marx Translation

January 5th. We had high and boisterous winds last night and this morning . . . In the first village there has been a buffalo-dance for the last three nights, which has put them all into commotion, and the description which we received from those of the party who visited the village, and from other sources, is not a little ludicrous.

The buffalo-dance is an institution originally intended for the benefit of the old men, and practiced at their suggestion. When buffalo become scarce they send a man to harangue the village, declaring that the game is far off and that a feast is necessary to bring it back and if the village be disposed a day and place is named for the celebration of it. At the appointed hour the old men arrive and seat themselves crosslegged on skins around a fire in the middle of the lodge with a sort of doll or small image, dressed like a female, placed before them. The young men bring them a platter of provisions, a pipe of tobacco, and their wives, whose dress on the occasion is only a robe or mantle loosely thrown around the body. On their arrival each youth selects the old man he means to distinguish by his favor and spreads before him the provisions, after which he presents the pipe and smokes with him. Next the old man shows the little girl doll. Then entering into an embrace, he throws it on the ground, and laying on it, hugs it with all the ardor of an old man. That's a sign. Then the wife leaves the crowd and with bodily motion cherishes the embrace of the old man lying on the ground. The husband draws near the old man with a sad face and begs him to preserve both his honor and dignity in the embrace of his wife. Perhaps at first the old man failed; then the husband pleads greatly with many prayers, tears, and gifts. Then the old lover, struck with mercy due to so many prayers, tears, and gifts, holds her in a mating embrace. He tries greatly, but riddled with age and weak, he tries in vain. Meanwhile the husband, standing nearby, rejoices greatly, his honor and dignity preserved. One of our men, much more hearty and potent, due to his youth, this night preserved the honor of four husbands.

Source: Walter H. Marx, "A Latin Matter in the Biddle 'Narrative' or 'History' of the Lewis and Clark Expedition," *We Proceeded On* IX, 4 (November 1983): 21–22.

Document 6
Meriwether Lewis, Fort Mandan, April 7, 1805

Having on this day at 4 P.M. completed every arrangement necessary for our departure, we dismissed the barge and crew with orders to return without loss of time to S. Louis, a small canoe with two French hunters accompanyed the barge; these men had assended the missouri with us the last year as engages. The barge crew consisted of six soldiers and two Frenchmen; two Frenchmen and a Ricara Indian also take their passage in her as far as the Ricara Vilages, at which place we expect Mr. Tiebeau [Tabeau] to embark with his peltry who in that case will make an addition of two, perhaps four men to the crew of the barge. We gave Richard Warfington, a discharged Corpl., the charge of the Barge and crew, and confided to his care likewise our dispatches to the government, letters to our private friends, and a number of articles to the President of the United States. One of the Frenchmen by the Name of Gravline an honest discrete man and an excellent boat-man is imployed to conduct the barge as a pilot; we have therefore every hope that the barge and with her our dispatches will arrive safe at St. Louis. Mr. Gravlin who speaks the Ricara language extreemly well, has been imployed to conduct a few of the Recara Chiefs to the seat of government who have promised us to decend in the barge to St. Liwis with that view.–

At same moment that the Barge departed from Fort Mandan, Capt. Clark embaked with our party and proceeded up the river. as I had used no exercise for several weeks, I determined to walk on shore as far as our encampment of this evening; accordingly I continued my walk on the N. side of the River about six miles, to the upper Village of the Mandans, and called on the Black Cat or Pose cop´se há, the great chief of the Mandans; he was not at home; I rested myself a minutes, and finding that the party had not arrived I returned about 2 miles and joined them at their encampment on the N. side of the river opposite the lower Mandan village. Our party now consisted of the following Individuals. Sergts. John Ordway, Nathaniel Prior, & Patric Gass; Privates, William Bratton, John Colter, Reubin, and Joseph Fields, John Shields, George Gibson, George Shannon, John Potts, John Collins, Joseph Whitehouse, Richard Windsor, Alexander Willard, Hugh Hall, Silas Goodrich, Robert Frazier, Peter Crouzatt, John Baptiest la Page, Francis Labiech, Hue McNeal, William Werner, Thomas P. Howard, Peter Wiser, and John B. Thompson.–

Interpreters, George Drewyer and Tauasant Charbono also a Black man by the name of York, servant to Capt. Clark, an Indian Woman wife to Charbono with a young child, and a Mandan man who had promised us to accompany us as far as the Snake Indians with a view to bring about a good understanding and friendly intercourse between that nation and his own, the Minetares and Ahwahharways.

Our vessels consisted of six small canoes, and two large perogues. This little fleet altho' not quite so rispectable as those of Columbus or Capt. Cook were still viewed by us with as much pleasure as those deservedly famed adventurers ever beheld theirs; and I dare say with quite as much anxiety for their safety and preservation. we were now about to penetrate a country at least two thousand miles in width, on which the foot of civillized man had never trodden; the good or evil it had in store for us was for experiment yet to determine, and these little vessells contained every article by which we were to expect to subsist or defend ourselves. however as this the state of mind in which we are, generally gives the colouring to events, when the immagination is suffered to wander into futurity, the picture which now presented itself to me was a most pleasing one. entertaining <now> as I do, the most confident hope of succeading in a voyage which had formed a da[r]ling project of mine for the last ten years <of my life>, I could but esteem this moment of my <our> departure as among the most happy of my life. The party are in excellent health and sperits, zealously attatched to the enterprise, and anxious to proceed; not a whisper of murmur or discontent to be heard among them, but all act in unison, and with the most perfect harmony. I took an early supper this evening and went to bed. Capt. Clark myself the two Interpretters and the woman and child sleep in a tent of dressed skins. this tent is in the Indian stile, formed of a number of dressed Buffaloe skins sewed together with sinues. it is cut in such a manner that when foalded double it forms the quarter of a circle, and is left open at one side where it may be attatched or loosened at pleasure by strings with are sewed to its sides to the purpose. to erect this tent, a parsel of ten or twelve poles are provided, fore or five of which are attatched together at one end, they are then elivated and their lower extremities are spread in a circular manner to a width proportionate to the demention of the lodge, in the same position orther poles are leant against those, and the leather is then thrown over them forming a conic figure.–

Source: Meriwether Lewis, Fort Mandan, April 7, 1805, in Gary E. Moulton, ed., *The Journals of the Lewis and Clark Expedition,* 13 vols. (Lincoln: University of Nebraska Press, 1983–2001), V, 118.

Document 7
Meriwether Lewis at the Great Falls of the Missouri, June 13, 1805

This morning we set out about sunrise after taking breakfast off our venison and fish. we again ascended the hills of the river and gained the level country. the country through which we passed for the first six miles tho' more roling than that we had passed yesterday might still with propryety be deemed a level country; our course as yesterday was generally SW. the river from the place we left it appeared to make a considerable bend to the South. from the extremity of this roling country I overlooked a most beatifull and level plain of great extent or at least 50 or sixty miles; in this there were infinitely more buffaloe than I had ever before witnessed at a view. nearly in the direction I had been travling or S. W. two curious mountains presented themselves of square figures, the sides rising perpendicularly to the hight of 250 feet and appeared to be formed of yellow clay; their tops appeared to be level plains; these inaccessible hights appeared like the ramparts of immence fortifications; I have no doubt but with very little assistance from art they might be rendered impregnable. fearing that the river boar to the South and that I might pass the falls if they existed between this an the snowey mountains I altered my course nealy to the South leaving those insulated hills to my wright and proceeded through the plain; I sent Feels on my right and Drewyer and Gibson on my left with orders to kill some meat and join me at the river where I should halt for dinner. I had proceded on this course about two miles with Goodrich at some distance behind me whin my ears were saluted with the agreeable sound of a fall of water and advancing a littler further I saw the spray arrise above the plain like a collumn of smoke which would frequently dispear again in an instant caused I presume by the wind which blew pretty hard from the S. W. I did not however loose my direction to this point which soon began to make a roaring too tremendious to be mistaken for any cause short of the great falls of the Missouri. here I arrived about 12 OClock having traveled by estimate about 15 Miles. I hurryed down the hill which was about 200 feet high and difficult of access, to gaze on this sublimely grand specticle. I took my position on the top of some rocks about 20 feet high opposite the center of the falls. this chain of rocks appear once to have formed a part of those over which the waters tumbled, but in the course of time has been seperated from it to the distance of 150 yards lying prarrallel to it and forming a butment against which the water after falling over the precipice beats with great fury; this barrier extends on the right to the perpendicular clift which forms that board of the river but to the distance of 120 yards next to the clift it is but a few feet above the level of the water, and here the way in very high tides appears to pass in a channel of 40 yds. next to the higher part of the ledg of rocks; on the left it extends within 80 or ninty yards of the lard. Clift which is also perpendicular; between this abrupt extremity of the ledge of rocks and the perpendicular bluff the whole body of water passes with incredible swiftness. immediately at the cascade the river is about 300 yds. wide; about ninty or a hundred yards of this next the Lard. bluff is a smoth even sheet of water falling over a precipice of at least eighty feet, the remaining part of about 200 yards on my right formes the grandest sight I ever beheld, the hight of the fall is the same of the other but the irregular and somewhat projecting rocks below receives the water in it's passage down and brakes it into a perfect white foam which assumes a thousand forms in a moment sometimes flying up in jets of sparkling foam to the hight of fifteen or twenty feet and are scarcely formed before large roling bodies of the same beaten and foaming water is thrown over and conceals them. in short the rocks seem to be most happily fixed to present a sheet of the whitest beaten froath for 200 yards in length and about 80 feet perpendicular. the water after decending strikes against the butment before mentioned or that on which I stand and seems to reverberate and being met by the more impetuous courant they role and swell into half formed billows of great hight which rise and again disappear in an instant. this butment of rock defends a handsom little bottom of about three acres which is deversified and agreeably shaded with some cottonwood trees; in the lower extremity of the bottom there is a very thick grove of the same kind of trees which are small, in this wood there are several Indian lodges formed of sticks. a few small cedar grow near the ledge of rocks where I rest. below the point of these rocks at a small distance the river is divided by a large rock which rises several feet above the water, and extends downwards with the stream for about 20 yards. about a mile before the water arrives at the pitch it decends very rappidly, and is confined on the Lard. side by a perpendicular clift of about 100 feet, on Stard. side it is also perpendicular for about three hundred yards above the pitch where it is then broken by the discharge of a small ravine, down which the buffaloe have a large beaten road to the water, for it is but in very few places that these anamals can obtain water near this place owing to the steep and inaccessible banks. I see several skelletons of the buffaloe lying in the edge of the water near the Stard. bluff which I presume have been swept down by the current and precipitated over this tremendious fall. about 300 yards below me there is another butment of solid rock with a perpendicular face and abot 60 feet high which projects from the Stard. side at right angles to the distance of 134 yds. and terminates the lower part nearly of the bottom before mentioned; there being a passage arround the end of this butment between it and the river of about 20 yardes; here the river again assumes it's usual width soon spreading to near 300 yards but still continues it's rappidity. from the reflection of the sun on the spray or mist which arrises from these falls there is a beatifull rainbow produced which adds not a little to the beauty of this majestically grand senery. after wrighting this

imperfect discription I again viewed the falls and was so much disgusted with the imperfect idea which it conveyed of the scene that I
determined to draw my pen across it and begin agin, but then reflected
that I could not perhaps succeed better than pening the first impres-
sions of the mind; I wished for the pencil of Salvator Rosa or the pen of
Thompson, that I might be enabled to give to the enlightened world
some just idea of this truly magnifficent and sublimely grand object,
which has from the commencement of time been concealed from the
view of civilized man; but this was fruitless and vain. I most sincerely
regreted that I had not brought a crimee obscura with me by the assistance of which even I could have hoped to have done better but alas
this was also out of my reach; I therefore with the assistance of my pen
only indeavoured to trace some of the stronger features of this seen by
the assistance of which and my recollection aided by some able pencil I
hope still to give to the world some faint idea of an object which at this
moment fills me with such pleasure and astonishment, and which of it's
kind I will venture to ascert is second to but one in the known world. I
retired to the shade of a tree where I determined to fix my camp for the
present and dispatch a man in the morning to inform Capt. C. and the
party of my success in finding the falls and settle in their minds all further doubts as to the Missouri . . .

   Goodrich had caught half a douzen very fine trout and a number
of both species of the white fish. these trout are from sixteen to twenty
three inches in length, precisely resemble our mountain or speckled
trout in form and the position of their fins, but the specks on these are
of a deep black instead of the red or goald colour of those common to
the U.' States. these are furnished long sharp teeth on the pallet and
tongue and have generally a small dash of red on each side behind the
front ventral fins; the flesh is of a pale yellowish red, or when in good
order, of a rose red.– . . .

   my fare is really sumptuous this evening; buffaloe's humps,
tongues and marrowbones, fine trout parched meal pepper and salt, and
a good appetite; the last is not considered the least of the luxuries.

Source: Lewis Meriwether, June 13, 1805, in Gary E. Moulton, ed., *The Journals
of the Lewis and Clark Expedition,* 13 vols. (Lincoln: University of Nebraska
Press, 1983–2001), 283–86.

Document 8
Meriwether Lewis, August 18, 1805

This day I completed my thirty first year, and conceived that I had in all human probability now existed about half the period which I am to remain in this Sublunary world. I reflected that I had as yet done but little, very little indeed, to further the hapiness of the human race, or to advance the information of the succeeding generation. I viewed with regret the many hours I have spent in indolence, and now soarly feel the want of that information which those hours would have given me had they been judiciously expended. but since they are past and cannot be recalled, I dash from me the gloomy thought and resolved in future, to redouble my exertions and at least indeavour to promote those two primary objects of human existence, by giving them the aid of that portion of talents which nature and fortune have bestoed on me; or in future, to live for *mankind,* as I have heretofore lived for *myself.–*

Source: Meriwether Lewis, August 18, 1805, in Gary E. Moulton, ed., *The Journals of the Lewis and Clark Expedition,* 13 vols. (Lincoln: University of Nebraska Press, 1983–2001), V, 118.

Document 9
Meriwether Lewis to Thomas Jefferson, St. Louis, September 23, 1806

Sir,

It is with pleasure that I anounce to you the safe arrival of myself and party at 12 OClk. today at this place with our papers and baggage. In obedience to your orders we have penitrated the Continent of North America to the Pacific Ocean, and sufficiently explored the interior of the country to affirm with confidence that we have discovered the most practicable rout which dose exist across the continent by means of the navigable branches of the Missouri and Columbia Rivers. Such is that by way of the Missouri to the foot of the rapids five miles below the great falls of that river a distance of 2575 miles, thence by land passing the Rocky Mountains to a navigable part of the Kooskooske 340; with the Kooskooske 73 mls. a South Easterly branch of the Columbia 154 miles and the latter river 413 mls. to the Pacific Ocean; making the total distance from the confluence of the Missouri and Mississippi to the discharge of the Columbia into the Pacific Ocean 3555 miles. The navigation of the Missouri may be deemed safe and good; it's difficulties arrise from it's falling banks, timber imbeded in the mud of it's channel, it's sand bars and steady rapidity of it's current, all which may be overcome with a great degree of certainty by taking the necessary precautions. The passage by land of 340 miles from the Missouri to the Kooskooske is the most formidable part of the tract proposed across the Continent; of this distance 200 miles is along a good road, and 140 over tremendious mountains which for 60 mls. are covered with eternal snows; however a passage over these mountains is practicable from the latter part of June to the last of September, and the cheep rate at which horses are to be obtained from the Indians of the Rocky Mountains and West of them, reduces the expences of transportation over this portage to a mere trifle. The navigation of the Kooskooske, the South East branch of the Columbia itself is safe and good from the 1st of April to the middle of August, by making three portages on the latter; the first of which in decending is that of 1200 paces at the great falls of the Columbia, 261 mls. from the Ocean, the second of two miles at the long narrows six miles below the falls, and the 3rd also of 2 miles at the great rapids 65 miles still lower down. The tides flow up the Columbia 183 miles, or within seven miles of the great rapids, thus far large sloops might ascend in safety, and vessels of 300 tons burthen could with equal safety reach the entrance of the river Multnomah, a large Southern branch of the Columbia, which taking it's rise on the confines of Mexico with the Callarado and Apostles river, discharges itself into the Columbia 125 miles from it's mouth. From the head of tide water to the foot of the long narrows the Columbia could be most advantageously navigated with large batteauxs, and from thence upwards by perogues. The Missouri possesses sufficient debth of water as far as is specifyed for boats of 15 tons burthen, but those of smaller capacity are to be prefered.

We view this passage across the Continent as affording immence advantages to the fur trade, but fear that the advantages which it offers as a communication for the productions of the Eeast Indies to the United States and thence to Europe will never be found equal on an extensive scale to that by way of the Cape of Good hope; still we believe that many articles not bulky brittle nor of very perishable nature may be conveyed to the United States by this rout with more facility and at less expence than by that at present practiced.

The Missouri and all it's branches from the Chyenne upwards abound more in beaver and Common Otter, than any other streams on earth, particularly that proportion of them lying within the Rocky Mountains. The furs of all this immence tract of country including such as may be collected on the upper portion of the River St. Peters, Red river and the Assinniboin with the immence country watered by the Columbia, may be conveyed to the mouth of the Columbia by the 1st of August in each year and from thence be shiped to, and arrive in Canton earlier thant he furs at present shiped from Montreal annually arrive in London. The British N. West Company of Canada were they permitted by the United States might also convey their furs collected in the Athabaske, on the Saskashawan, and South and West of Lake Winnipic by that rout within the period before mentioned. Thus the productions [of] nine tenths of the most valuable fur country of America could be conveyed by the rout proposed to the East Indies.

In the infancy of the trade across the continent, or during the period that the trading establishments shall be confined to the Missouri and it's branches, the men employed in this trade will be compelled to convey the furs collected in that quarter as low on the Columbia as tide water, in which case they could not return to the falls of the Missouri untill about the 1st of October, which would be so late in the season that there would be considerable danger of the river being obstructed by ice before they could reach this place and consequently that the comodites brought from the East indies would be detained untill the following spring; but this difficulty will at once vanish when establishments are also made on the Columbia, and a sufficient number of men employed at them to convey annually the productions of the East indies to the upper establishment on the Kooskooske, and there exchange them with the men of the Missouri for their furs, in the begining of July. By this means the furs not only of the Missouri but those also of the Columbia may be shiped to the East indies by the season before mentioned, and the comodities of the East indies arrive at St. Louis or the mouth of the Ohio by the last of September in each year.

Although the Columbia dose not as much as the Missouri abound in beaver and Otter, yet it is by no means despicable in this rispect, and would furnish a valuable fur trade distinct from any other consideration in addition to the otter and beaver which it could furnish. There might be collected considerable quantities of the skins of three speceis of bear affording a great variety of colours and of superior delicacy, those also of the tyger cat, several species of fox, martin and several others of an inferior class of furs, besides the valuable Sea Otter of the coast.

If the government will only aid, even in a very limited manner, the enterprize of her Citizens I am fully convinced that we shal shortly derive the benifits of a most lucrative trade from this source, and that in the course of ten or twelve years a tour across the Continent by the rout mentioned will be undertaken by individuals with as little concern as a voyage across the Atlantic is at present.

The British N. West Company of Canada has for several years, carried on a partial trade with the Minnetares Ahwayhaways and Mandans on the Missouri from their establishments on the Assinniboin at the entrance of Mouse river; at present I have good reason for beleiving that they intend shortly to form an establishment near those nations with a view to engroce the fur trade of the Missouri. The known enterprize and resources of this Company, latterly strengthened by an union with their powerfull rival the X. Y. Company renders them formidable in that distant part of the continent to all other traders; and in my opinion if we are to regard the trade of the Missouri as an object of importance to the United States; the strides of this Company towards the Missouri cannot be too vigilantly watched nor too firmly and speedily opposed by our government. The embarrasments under which the naviagation of the Missouri at present labours from the unfriendly dispositions of the Kancez, the several bands of Tetons, Assinniboins and those tribes that resort to the British establishments on the Saskashawan is also a subject which requires the earliest attention of our government. As I shall shortly be with you I have deemed it unnecessary here to detail the several ideas which have presented themselves to my mind on those subjects, more especially when I consider that a thorough knowledge of the geography of the country is absolutely necessary to their being unde[r]stood, and leasure has not yet permited us to make but one general map of the country which I am unwilling to wrisk by the Mail.

As a sketch of the most prominent features of our perigrination since we left the Mandans may not be uninteresting, I shall indeavour to give it to you by way of letter from this place, where I shall necessarily be detained several days in order to settle with and discharge the men who accompanyed me on the voyage as well as to prepare for my rout to the City of Washington.

We left Fort Clatsop where we wintered near the entrance of the Columbia on the 27th of March last, and arrived at the foot of the Rocky mountains on the 10th of May where we were detained untill the 24th of June in consequence of the snow which rendered a passage over the those Mountains impracticable untill that moment; had it not been for this detention I should ere this have joined you at Montichello. In my last communication to you from the Mandans I mentioned my intention of sending back a canoe with a small party from the Rocky Mountains; but on our arrival at the great falls of the Missouri on the 14th of June 1805, in view of that formidable snowey barrier, the discourageing difficulties which we had to encounter in making a portage of eighteen miles of our canoes and baggage around those falls were such that my friend Capt. Clark and myself conceived it inexpedient to reduce the party, lest by doing so we should lesson the ardor of those who remained and thus hazard the fate of the expedition, and therefore declined that measure, thinking it better that the government as well as our friends should for a moment feel some anxiety for our fate than to wrisk so much; experience has since proved the justice of our dicision, for we have more than once owed our lives and the fate of the expedition to our number which consisted of 31 men.

I have brought with me several skins of the Sea Otter, two skins of the native sheep of America, five skins and skelitons complete of the Bighorn or mountain ram, and a skin of the Mule deer beside the skins of several other quadrupeds and birds natives of the countries through which we have passed. I have also preserved a pretty extensive collection of plants, and collected nine other vocabularies.

I have prevailed on the great Cheif of the Mandan nation to accompany me to Washington; he is now with my frind and colligue Capt. Clark at this place, in good health and sperits, and very anxious to proceede.

With rispect to the exertions and services rendered by that esteemable man Capt. William Clark in the course of late voyage I cannot say too much; if sir any credit be due for the success of that arduous enterprize in which we have been mutually engaged, he is equally with myself entitled to your consideration and that of our common country.

The anxiety which I feel in returning once more to the bosom of my friends is a sufficient guarantee that no time will be unnecessarily expended in this quarter.

I have detained the post several hours for the purpose of making you this haisty communication. I hope that while I am pardoned for this detention of the mail, the situation in which I have been compelled to write will sufficiently apologize for having been this laconic.

The rout by which I purpose traveling from hence to Washington is by way of Cahokia, Vincennes, Louisvill Ky., the Crab orchard, Abington, Fincastle, Stanton and Charlottsville. Any letters directed to me at Louisville ten days after the receipt of this will most probably meet me at that place. I am very anxious to learn of the state of my friends in Albemarle particularly whether my mother is yet living. I am with every sentiment of esteem Your Obt. and very Humble servent.

MERIWETHER LEWIS Capt.
1st U.S. Regt. Infty.

N.B. The whole of the party who accompanyed me from the Mandans have returned in good health, which is not, I assure you, to me one of the least pleasing considerations of the Voyage.

M. L.

Source: Lewis to Jefferson, St. Louis, September 23, 1806, in Donald Jackson, ed., *Letters of the Lewis and Clark Expedition, with Related Documents, 1783–1854,* 2nd ed., 2 vols. (Urbana: University of Illinois Press, 1978), I, 319–24.

Document 10
Lewis to an Unknown Correspondent, Cahokia, October 14, 1806

Sketch of Captn. Lewis's Voyage to the Pacific Ocean by the Missesourii & Columbia Rivers from the States of America.
Dear Sir,

Annexed is the sketch I mentioned to you in my last of the 7th inst. I will give it you verbatim.

Cahokia 14th Oct. 1806

Dear Sir,   St. Louis 29th Sept. 1806

I arrived here the 23rd instant from the Pacific Ocean where I remained during the last winter, near the entrance of the Columbia River–This Station we left the 23rd March last and should have reached

St. Louis early in August had we not been detained by snows which buried the passage of the Rocky Mountains until the 26th June, even at this late season, strange as it may appear to an inhabitant of the southern States, we were compelled to travel over snows from 4 to 6 feet for the distance of 60 miles–In returning thro' the Rocky Mountains, we divided ourselves into several parties digressing from the Route by which we went out with a view more effectually to explore the Country, and discover the most practicable Route which existed across the continent by way of the Missesouris & Columbia Rivers: in this we have been completely successful. Therefore have no hesitation to say & declare, that such as Nature has permitted we have discovered the most practicable Route which does exist across the Continent of North America in that direction; such is that by way of the Missesourii to the foot of the Rapids below the great Falls of that River a distance of 2575 miles, thence by land passing the Rocky Mountains to a navigable part of the Kooskooskee 320 M. & the Kooskooskee 73 M. Lewis River 152 M. & the Columbia 413 M. to the Pacific Ocean making the total Distance from the confluence of the Missesourii & Mississippi to the discharge of the Columbia into the Pacific Ocean 3555 miles.–The navigation of the Missesourii may be deemed good, it's difficulties arise from it's falling Banks, Timbers imbedded in the Mud of it's channels, it's sand Bars, & steady rapidity of it's Current, all which may be overcome with a great degree of certainty by taking the necessary precautions–The Passage of 320 M. from the Missesourii to the Kooskooskee is the most formidable part of the Track proposed across the Continent, of this distance 200 M. is along a good Road and 140 M. over tremendous Mountains, which for 60 miles are covered with eternal Snows; however a passage over those Mountains is practicable from the latter part of June to the last of September. The cheap rate at which Horses are to be obtained from the Indians of the Rocky Mountains & west of them, reduces the Expences of Transportation over this Passage to a mere Trifle. The Navigation of the Kooskooskee, Louise Rivers & Columbia safe and good from the 9th April to the middle of August, by making three Portages in the Columbia; the first of which in descending that River is of 1200 Paces at the Falls of that River 261 Miles from the Ocean. The second of 2 miles at the long Narrows, 6 M. below the Falls, the third also of 2 Miles 65 Miles still lower down. The Tides flow up the Columbia 183 Miles, thus far large Sloops might ascend in safety

& vessels of 300 Tons could with equal safety reach the Entrance of Multnomack River, a large southern Branch of the Columbia, which taking it's rise on the confines of Mexico with the Collarado & Apostles River discharges itself into the Columbia 25 M. from it's Mouth.–I consider this Track across the Continent as presenting immense advantages to the Fur Trade–as all the Furs collected in 9/10 of the valuable Fur Country of America may be conveyed to the Mouth of the Columbia & shipped from thence for the East Indies by the 1st of August in each year, & will of course reach Canton earlier than the Furs which are annually exported from Montreal reach Great Britain.

In our outward bound Voyage we ascended the Missesourii to the Foot of the Rapids 5 Miles below the great Falls, where we arrived the 14th June 1805 not having then met with any of the Natives of the Rocky Mountains, we were of course ignorant of the passes by Land across these Mountains, & even had we known them, we were destitute of Horses; which were absolutely necessary to enable us to transport the requisite quantity of ammunition & other stores to insure the success of the remaining part of the Voyage down the Columbia, we therefore determined to navigate the Missesourii as far as it was practicable, or until we met some of the Natives from whom we could obtain Horses & the requisite Information with respect to the Country; accordingly we undertook a most laborious Portage of our Canoes & Baggage, around the Falls of the Missesourii of 16 Miles which we finally effected the 3rd July, from hence ascending the Missesourii, we entered the Rocky Mountains at the distance of 71 Miles farther, here the Missesourii divides itself into 3 nearly equal Branches. At the same point, the two largest Branches are so nearly of the same dignity that we did not conceive that either of them could with propriety retain the name of Missesourii, & therefore we call them, Jefferson's, Maddison's & Gallatin's River; the confluence of these Rivers may properly be deemed the Head of that majestic River the Missesourii & to it's Forks is 2848 Miles from it's Junction with the Mississippi. We arrived at the Head of the Missesourii the 27 July 1805 not having yet been so fortunate as to meet with the Natives altho' Capt. Clark had previously made several excursions since we had entered the Mountains for that Purpose–We were compelled still to continue our route by water. The most northward of the 3 Forks, that which we had given the name Jefferson's River was deemed the most proper for our purpose accordingly we ascended it

248 Miles to it's upper Forks, being it's extreme navigable Point making the distance to which we had navigated the waters of the Missesourii 3096 Miles of which 429 lay within the Mountains. On the evening of 16th August at the upper Forks of Jefferson's River having previously with a Party of 3 men ascended the main Fork of Jefferson's River to it's extreme Fountain, passed the Rocky Mountains to the Natives of Columbia, discovered a Band of Shoshones, who were in Possession of an abundance of Horses, & found means to prevail on 34 of their principal Chiefs & Warriors to accompany me to that place; here I was joined early in the morning of the 17th by Capt. Clark & Party with our Canoes & Baggage. From the Natives we now learned that the River on which they reside was not navigable, & that a Passage thro' the Mountains in that direction was impracticable; being unwilling to confide implicitly in this unfavourable account of the Natives, it was concerted between Capt. Clark & myself that he should go forward immediately with a small party and explore the River, while I in the interim would lay up the Canoes at that place & engage the Shoshones with their Horses to assist in transporting our Baggage over the Mountains to their Camp, a distance of 45 Miles, accordingly he set out early next morning, passed the dividing Mountains between the waters of the Missesourii & Columbia Rivers, & descended that Branch of the little River about 70 Miles; finding the indian account of the Country in the direction of that River correct, he returned & joined me at the Shoshones Camp on the 27th August excessively fatigued, having been compelled to subsist on Berries during the greater part of his Route; we now purchased 27 Horses of these Indians, and engaged a Guide to conduct us. The Guide informed us he would in 15 days take us to a large River in an open level Country, west of these Mountains by a Route some distance to the north of the River on which they lived & that by which the natives west of the Mountains visited the Plains of the Missesourii for the purpose of hunting the Buffalo, pleased with this Information, after doubting from our observations as well as the corroborating testimony of many Indians that a passage was practicable thro' those Mountains to the west, we hastened the preparations for our departure & set forward with our Guide 31st August depending principally for subsistance on our pack Horses already heavily laden with Ammunition & other Stores necessary to the successful prosecution of our voyage beyond the Mountains, which of course we should have been compelled to deposit as we

killed the Horses that transported them. Thus situated we attempted with success those unknown formidable snow clad Mountains on the bare word of a Savage, while 99/100th of his Countrymen assured us that a passage was impracticable, most fortunately on our way within the Mountains we met with a travelling Band of the Tushopahs going to the Plains of the Missesourii in quest of Buffaloe & obtained from them an accession of 7 Horses to our former Stock exchanging at the same time 10 or 12 to great advantage; this ultimately proved of infinite Service to us as we were compelled to subsist on Horse Beef & Dogs previous to our arrival in the navigable [part?] of the Kooskooskee. I have not leisure at this moment to state all those difficulties which we encountered in our Passage over these Mountains—suffice it to say we suffered everything Cold, Hunger & Fatigue could impart, or the Keenest Anxiety excited for the fate of Expedition in which our whole Souls were embarked. Our difficulties with respect to Provisions did not cease on our arrival at the Kooskooskee 24th Sept 1805 altho' the Pallotepalless a numerous People enhabiting that Country, extremely friendly & for a few paltry articles furnished us with an abundance of Provisions such as they were accustomed to themselves, consisting of dried Salmon & Roots; we found in experiment that we could not subsist on it, and grew sick on eating those Articles & we were obliged to have recourse to the Flesh of Horses, Dogs & to supply the deficiency of our Guns, which produced but little meat as Game was scarce in the vicinity of our Camp on the Kooskooskee, where we were compelled to remain in order to construct Pirogues for the purpose of descending the River. At this season the Salmon altho' abundant are so meagre that they are unfit for use in great measure—During our residence at this compound we were all Sick—for my own part I suffered a severe Indisposition for 10 or 12 days, thus sick feeble & emaciated, we commenced & continued the operation of building four large Pirogues & a small Canoe, which we finally completed on the 6th October—The next day we delivered our Horses in charge to the Pallotepalless until our Return, & embarked ourselves & Baggage aboard our Pirogues & Canoe for the Pacific Ocean, descending by that Route already mentioned; the water of the River being low at this season we experienced much difficulty in descending—we found the Channels obstructed by a great number of dangerous rapids in passing across which our Pirogues several times foundered on the Rocks the Crew narrowly escaped with their Lives;

this difficulty however does not exist in the high Water which happens within the Period previously mentioned; in this State the Current is not so great as that of the Missesourii in the Spring Tides–On this portion of our Route we found the Natives extremely numerous & generally friendly, tho' we have on several occasions owed our Lives & consequently the final success of the Expedition to our Number which consisted of 31 Men–On the 17th November we reached the Pacific Ocean where various considerations induced us to spend the last Winter; we therefore searched for an eligible situation for that purpose & slected a Spit on the south Shore of a little River called by the Natives Netit which discharges itself into a small Bay S.E. side of the Columbia 14 miles within point Adams. Here we constructed some Log Houses & defended them by a common Stockade Work, this Place we called Fort Clatsop after a Nation of that Name, who were our nearest neighbors, it is 7 miles distant from the Ocean on a direct Line, & 3 Miles from the discharge of the Netit near Fort Clatsop–We found an abundance of Elk on which we subsisted principally during the Winter at the Ocean. We made a sufficient quantity of Salt to supply our wants until our return to our deposit of that Article on the Missesourii–During our residence at this place we saw no trading vessels, but we had abundant Proofs there are 11 or 12 vessels which annually enter the River for the purpose of trading with the Natives.–These people gave us the Names of 12 Commanders of Vessels 11 of whom they informed us, visited them once & sometimes twice a year all these names are English or American as Haley, More, Davidsons. The Natives never attempted to speak the Language of any other civilized Nation except that of the English–many words of which they pronounce distinctly–I believe these Traders to be for the most part Americans, if not exclusively so–We learned nothing of the state of the Settlement of Nootka Sound. On our homeward bound Journey, being much better acquainted with the Country we were enabled to take such precautions as did in a great Measure secure us from the want of Provisions, & lessens our fatigues infinitely when compared to those to which we were exposed when we went out–Within the Rocky Mountains Capt. Clark & myself separated, he travelled in the first Instance tot he Forts [forks] of Jefferson's River where we had laid up the Canoes in August 1805, & myself directly to the Falls of Missesourii, both without Guides & by Routes which we had never previously travelled & yet we both succeeded beyond our

Expectations & reached our place of destination without any difficulty of consequence–Capt. Clark having descended Jefferson's River to it's confluence with Maddison's & Gallatin's Rivers dispatched the Canoes with a Party under the command of Serjeant John Otway [Ordway] to the entrance of the River Maria a large northern branch of the Missesourii which taking it's rise in the Rocky Mountains adjacent to the Saskatchewan River, discharges itself [ ] Miles below the Falls of the Missessourii, to the Yellowstone River a distance of 48 Miles, where that River issues from the Mountains, & from whence it is navigable to the Missesourii 817 Miles, not finding Timber in the Yellowstone River to sufficient Size to construct Canoes–Capt. Clark & Party travelled down it by land 115 Miles when finding Timber proper for his purpose he built 2 small Canoes & descended without difficulty to the Missessourii from the point at which Capt. Clark constructed those Canoes.–He dispatched Serjeant Nat Pryer with 3 men & Horses by Land to the Mandans in order to carry into execution certain arrangements which we had made in relation to Sicoux's but unfortunately the second evening after Serjeant Pryer had separated from Capt. Clark on the 25 July last the Natives stole his Horses & he was compelled to return with his small Party to the Yellowstone River where he formed Canoes of Skins of Buffaloes, descended the River & overtook Capt. Clark on the Missesourii the 8th August.–In the meantime I had passed with the remainder of the party to the upper part of the Portage near the great Falls of the Missesourii & explored the Medicine River from the Rocky Mountains to it's discharge in the Missesourii on the north side near that place.

I had now in conformity to my plan to undertake another enterprise which was to explore the River Maria completely with a view to establish, provided it so existed that some of it's Branches extended so far north as Lat 49° 37′ N on the same parallel of Lat with the N W extremity of the Lake of the Woods. The entrance of the River Maria I had previously ascertained to be 27° 25′ 17″ N & from the rise of that River as well as the direction it first takes, there were good grounds to hope that it extended to Lat 49° 37′ N believing it of the highest national importance as it respects our Treaty of 1783 with Great Britain. To establish that, I determined to execute it at every hazard & for that purpose I had brought with me a set of excellent Horses from the Plains of the Columbia west of the Rocky Mountains–I was well apprised that the Country thro' which it became necessary for me to pass was inhabited by several large & roving Bands of the Minnitares & Black Foot Indians, who trade at the British Settlements on the Saskoohawan, & from whom should I meet them I could have but little to hope from their friendship–unfortunately for me on the 11 July the day of my arrival at the upper part of the Portage on Missesourii, the Indians, believed to be the Tushopahs stole 7 of my best Horses, this accident compelled me not only to take my Route to the River Maria on inferior Horses, but also to reduce my Escort from 6 to 3 only–having left Serjeant Pat Glass [Gass] with 5 Men & 4 Horses at the Portage to make necessary preparations in order to facilitate the transportation of the Canoes & Baggage overland when they should arrive–I selected Geo Droulliard, Ruben & Jos Fields to accompany me, these were three of the most active resolute young Men which I had & the best marksmen–with these Men I quitted my Station at the Portage of the Missesourii on the 17 July & explored, with all it's Branches to the Rocky Mountains, being fully satisfied that no branch of this River extended so far North as Lat. 49. 37–I set out on my return on the 20th of the same Month met with a party of Minnitaries, these people appeared extremely friendly on our first interview & insisted on remaining with us all that night to which I consented. Early in the morning of the 27th they treacherously seized on & made themselves masters of all our Guns–in which Situation we engaged them with our Knives & our Pistol recovered our Guns & killed 2 of them & put the others to flight, pursued them retook our Horses, excepting 2 which they had attempted to carry off & took from them 15 Horses, a Gun and Several Bows & Quivers of Arrows, Shields & all their Baggage–fearing pursuit from 2 large Bands whom the Indians had informed us on the evening before were in our neighborhood, we hastened to the confluence of the Rivers Maria & Missesourii where I had appointed the Canoes & Party to meet me–at 8 o'clock on the 28th I arrived on the Bank of the Missesourii about 15 Miles above it's Junction witht the River Maria & met accidently with the Canoes & Party descending. I now dismissed my Horses & embarked having travelled from 6 o'clock in the morning of the 27th to the time I met the Canoes 142 Miles–We now continued our Route down the Missesourii without interruption or material accident until the 11th August, when going in there with one of my Hunters to kill some Elk he mistook me from the colour of my Dress which was leather from an Elk fired on me & hit me thro' the upper part of my thigh fortunately the Ball missed the bone & being in a good State of Health I recovered rapidly & by the 7 Sept was able to walk with tolerable convenience, having since fully recovered.–On the 12 August I overtook Capt. Clark & Party on the Missesourii 130 Miles above the Mandans, here we found ourselves once more all together and descended in safety to this Place, where we arrived as has been before mentioned on the 23rd Instant in perfect Health.

Source: Lewis to an Unknown Correspondent, Cahokia, October 14, 1806, in Donald Jackson, ed., *Letters of the Lewis and Clark Expedition, with Related Documents, 1783–1854,* 2nd ed., 2 vols. (Urbana: University of Illinois Press, 1978), I, 225–42.

GLOSSARY OF SELECTED TERMS

American Philosophical Society: Founded by Benjamin Franklin in Philadelphia in 1743 "for the promotion of useful knowledge." Thomas Jefferson was president, 1797–1815. The scientists who helped Meriwether Lewis prepare for the Expedition were all members. Since 1817 it has been the main repository for the original journals of Lewis and Clark.

Blackfeet Indians: The American Blackfeet are Piegan or Pikuni; Canadian sub-tribes are Kainah, or Blood, and Siksika. Members of the Algonquian linguistic family, they arrived on the Northern Plains about 1750 and soon acquired horses, then guns. At the time of Lewis and Clark they were the dominant tribe on the Northern Plains.

Camp Chopunnish: Lewis and Clark campsite, May 14–June 10, 1806, on the east bank of the Clearwater River at modern Kamiah, Idaho. Lewis and Clark called the Nez Perce the Chopunnish Indians. Elliott Coues named the campsite in 1893.

Camp Disappointment: Meriwether Lewis campsite, July 20–26, 1806, on Cut Bank Creek in the present Blackfeet Indian Reservation, the northernmost point reached by the Expedition. Named by Lewis because the Marias River flowed from the west, not the north as hoped, and because the weather was too cloudy to take celestial observations.

Camp Dubois: Corps of Discovery campsite for 152 days, December 13, 1803–May 14, 1804, at the mouth of the Wood River in Illinois Territory. Here the shakedown phase of the Expedition occurred—organization, drill, discipline, planning, and packing.

Camp Fortunate: Lewis and Clark campsite, August 16–24, 1805, at the confluence of Red Rock River and Horse Prairie Creek, the headwaters of the Beaverhead River in southwestern Montana. Named because there the Shoshoni chief Cameahwait was reunited with his sister Sacagawea. Now inundated by the Clark Canyon Reservoir.

Celilo Falls: The Great Falls of the Columbia River, about 4.5 miles below the mouth of the Deschutes River. "The whole height of the falls is 37 feet 8 inches, in a distance of 1,200 yards." The central marketplace of the Columbia basin and a favorite fishing site of the Wishram and Wasco Indians. Now inundated under the waters behind The Dalles Dam, since 1957.

Columbia River: The "Great River of the West," originating in British Columbia and flowing 1,214 miles to the Pacific. Discovered in 1775 by Bruno Hezeta of Spain, although not entered until 1792 by Robert Gray of Boston, who named it after his ship, the *Columbia Rediviva*. Navigated to the Willamette by W. R. Broughton of Britain in 1792. Explored from the Yakima River to its mouth, about 335 miles, by Lewis and Clark in 1805–1806.

Continental Divide: A natural watershed in the Rocky Mountains, separating rivers flowing east into, ultimately, the Gulf of Mexico and west into the Pacific Ocean.

The Dalles: Literally, from the French, "gutter stones," or flagstones, describing the chunks of lava sprinkled across the Columbia river bed about 190–200 miles from the bar. Also, the Short and Long Narrows. The "Short Narrows" are one-quarter mile long and 45 yards wide; the "Long Narrows" are five miles long and 200 yards wide.

Enlightenment: An eighteenth-century Atlantic intellectual movement centering on science, nature, law, political theory, and philosophy. Enlightened thinkers questioned received authority and, through reason, sought to expand the bounds of knowledge. They thought they might discover "natural law," the way the world works, in physical and human behavior alike. Benjamin Franklin, Thomas Jefferson, David Rittenhouse, and Thomas Paine are American Enlightenment figures.

Flathead Indians: A Salishan tribe, encountered by the Expedition on September 4, 1805, on the East Fork of the Bitterroot River. Also: Tushepau, Eoote-lash-Schute. Called "flathead" because they did not deform their foreheads; we are all flatheads. "33 Lodges about 80 men 400 Total and at least 500 horses" (Clark). "They talk as though they lisped or have a bur on their tongue. we Suppose that they are the welch Indians" (Ordway). *Journals,* V, 187; IX, 218.

Fort Clatsop: Winter campsite of the Expedition, December 7, 1805–March 23, 1806. On the west bank of the Netul (now Lewis and Clark) River, near Young's Bay, about five miles from modern Astoria, Oregon. Named for the local Indian tribe.

Fort Mandan: Winter campsite of the Expedition, November 3, 1804–April 7, 1805, on the east bank of the Missouri River, across the river and about two miles east of Chief Sheheke's Mandan village, near the mouth of the Knife River at modern Washburn, North Dakota.

Fort Massac: A French (1757), British (1763), and American (1794) military post on the Ohio River near Metropolis, Illinois. Visited by Lewis and Clark, November 11–13, 1803. George Drouillard and Private Joseph Whitehouse joined the Expedition here.

Great Falls of the Missouri: In aptly named Cascade County, Montana, there are actually five separate falls in a 10-mile stretch, with intervening rapids: the Great Falls, reached by Meriwether Lewis on June 13, 1805, and, proceeding upriver, Crooked Falls, Rainbow Falls, Colter Falls, and Black Eagle Falls. The Expedition's portage around these falls took 32 days. "Nowhere in the entire length of the river," writes Bernard DeVoto, "has industrial civilization . . . more hideously defaced the scene than a power development has done here" (*The Course of Empire* [Boston: Houghton Mifflin, 1952], 487).

Harpers Ferry: A federal armory in Virginia (now West Virginia) completed in 1801. Meriwether Lewis ordered the Expedition's weapons here and picked them up in early July 1803. The armory, at the confluence of the Shenandoah and Potomac Rivers, became a center of interchangeable-parts technology and the site of John Brown's raid (1859) and Stonewall Jackson's attack (1862).

Hidatsa Indians: Plains tribe living near the mouth of the Knife River in modern North Dakota. Three Hidatsa villages and two Mandan sites made up this complex. The Hidatsas knew the geography of the Northern Plains; one war chief "gave us a Chart in his way of the Missourie," reported Clark (*Journals,* III, 276). Also called Minitaris, or Gros Ventres.

Louisiana Purchase: In the greatest real estate transaction in American history, the Jefferson administration acquired Louisiana Territory from France in 1803. France sold all the western drainages of the Mississippi River plus the city of New Orleans for $15 million. West Florida, in dispute, was annexed by the U.S. in 1812. By further treaty in 1818 the northern border was set at the 49th Parallel, and in 1819 the western boundary at the Sabine River, excluding Texas. The land sale doubled the size of the United States.

Alexander Mackenzie, 1763–1820: A Scottish fur trader in the employ of the North West Company, he traveled down the river that bears his name to the Arctic Ocean in 1789. Four years later he became the first known European to cross North America north of Mexico. He went down the Fraser River until it became impassable, then overland to the Pacific coast at Bella Coola. He painted a rock: "Alexander Mackenzie, from Canada, by land, the twenty-second of July, one thousand seven hundred and ninety-three."

Mandan Indians: Plains Indians living in two towns along the Missouri River near the mouth of the Knife in modern North Dakota. Lewis and Clark wintered near the village of Mitutanka in 1804–1805. The Mandans were agriculturalists and traders. Their principal chiefs were Black Cat and Sheheke.

Marias River: Unexpected tributary of the Missouri, reached by Lewis and Clark on June 2, 1805. Turbulent, muddy, and running high, the river baffled the explorers for one solid week. Lewis named it Maria's River, "in honour of Miss Maria W—d" (a cousin). "It is true that the hue of the waters of this turbulent and troubled stream but illy comport with the pure celestial virtues and amiable qualifications of that lovely fair one; but on the other hand it is a noble river" (*Journals,* IV, 266).

Nez Perce Indians: Plateau tribe living along the Clearwater River in modern Idaho when encountered by Lewis and Clark in September 1805. "Nez Perce" is French for "pierced nose," although the Nez Perce did not pierce their noses in the nineteenth century (they may have earlier). The name may derive from sign language for Ne-mee-poo, "the people" (a pointed finger drawn across the face). Lewis and Clark called them "Chopunnish," which may mean "piercing." The Nez Perce nurtured the party back to health, provided guides down the Snake and Colombia, and kept the party's horses over the winter.

Nine Young Men from Kentucky: Sergeants Charles Floyd and Nathaniel Pryor; Privates William Bratton, John Colter, Reubin Field, Joseph Field, George Gibson, George Shannon, and John Shields.

Rocky Mountains: The American segment of the great rib of the Western Hemisphere, running from Alaska to the tip of South America. The Rockies are not a single chain but dozens of interlocking chains, which posed a tremendous geographical challenge to Lewis and Clark. Saddle Mountain, at 8,482 feet, near Lost Trail Pass, is the highest elevation reached by the Expedition.

Shoshoni Indians: Plateau tribe first encountered by Meriwether Lewis on August 13, 1805, on the Lemhi River in Idaho. The Shoshoni had been the first Northern Plains tribe to acquire horses (from Spanish herds in the Southwest), but Blackfeet guns had driven them into the mountains. They still hunted seasonally on the plains, but risked attack; in one Hidatsa raid about 1799, Sacagawea was abducted. Her brother was Chief Cameahwait. One of the pivotal tribes on the Expedition.

Sioux Indians: The most numerous (about 30,000) plains tribe, stretching from Minnesota to Montana and Canada to the Platte River. Divided into numerous bands: Santee, Yankton, Tetons, Oglalas, Brules, Sans Arc, Minniconjou, Hunkpapa. Lewis and Clark met the Yanktons and the Tetons coming up the Missouri River in 1804.

Snake River: At 1,000 miles, the 11th-longest river in the United States, originating in Yellowstone National Park, describing a huge arc across southern Idaho, and emptying into the Columbia near Pasco, Washington. Cameahwait described this river to Meriwether Lewis, but he dismissed its route as too roundabout. Also: Lewis's River, South Fork of the Columbia.

Three Forks: Headwaters of the Missouri River; the confluence of the Jefferson, Madison, and Gallatin Rivers. "An essential point in the geography of this western part of the Continent" for Meriwether Lewis, who arrived there on July 27, 1805 (*Journals*, IV, 435).

Travellers Rest: Lewis and Clark campsite (September 9–11, 1805, and June 30–July 3, 1806) near the mouth of Lolo Creek, about eight miles south of modern Missoula, Montana. Here Meriwether Lewis learned of an overland shortcut to the Missouri River, a route he followed on his return trip. Named by Lewis after a crossroads in northwestern South Carolina.

Treaty of San Ildefonso: October 1, 1800; France reacquired Louisiana from Spain. This diplomatic transaction set in motion the American purchase of Louisiana and the Expedition of Lewis and Clark.

ANNOTATED BIBLIOGRAPHY

The Journals of Lewis and Clark

Bergon, Frank, ed. *The Journals of Lewis and Clark.* New York: Penguin Books, 1989. Another abridged edition, with more natural and scientific history.

[Biddle, Nicholas, ed.]. *History of the Expedition under the Command of Captains Lewis and Clark, to the Sources of the Missouri, thence across the Rocky Mountains and down the River Columbia to the Pacific Ocean. Performed during the Years 1804–5–6 by Order of the Government of the United State.* Prepared for the press by Paul Allen, Esq. 2 vols. Philadelphia: Bradford and Inskeep, 1814. Biddle, a Philadelphia litterateur, paraphrased the narrative, omitting most scientific information. Clark and Private George Shannon answered his questions. Exceedingly rare, this edition has been reprinted many times in the twentieth century, most recently in 3 vols., Philadelphia: J. B. Lippincott, 1961.

Coues, Elliott. ed. *History of the Expedition under the Command of Captains Lewis and Clark . . .* 4 vols. New York: Francis P. Harper, 1893. Reprint (in 3 vols.), New York: Dover Publications, 1964. A reprint, still available in paperback, of the Biddle edition. Coues (pronounced "cows"), a naturalist, added extensive scientific annotation.

Cutright, Paul Russell. *A History of the Lewis and Clark Journals.* Norman: University of Oklahoma Press, 1976. The fascinating story of the provenance of the journals, new discoveries, and publication histories.

DeVoto, Bernard, ed. *The Journals of Lewis and Clark.* Boston: Houghton Mifflin, 1953. An abridged one-volume edition of Thwaites's original journals, with an excellent introduction. DeVoto was a popularizer of the Expedition. Still in print after half a century.

MacGregor, Carol Lynn, ed. *The Journals of Patrick Gass: Member of the Lewis and Clark Expedition.* Missoula, Mont.: Mountain Press, 1997. The first separate publication of Sergeant Gass's journal since 1807.

Moulton, Gary E., ed. *The Journals of the Lewis and Clark Expedition.* 13 vols. Lincoln: University of Nebraska Press, 1983–2001. Moulton set out to incorporate all the scattered journal publications in a comprehensive edition, thoroughly annotated, and subjected to modern editorial standards. Vol. 1 is an atlas, Vol. 12 an herbarium, and Vol. 13 an index. The standard reference for the twenty-first century.

Osgood, Ernest Staples, ed. *The Field Notes of Captain William Clark, 1803–1805.* New Haven, Conn.: Yale University Press, 1964. Facsimiles and transcripts of notes discovered in an attic in Minneapolis in 1953.

Quaife, Milo M., ed. *The Journals of Captain Meriwether Lewis and Sergeant John Ordway, Kept on the Expedition of Western Exploration, 1803–1806.* Madison, Wisc.: The State Historical Society of Wisconsin, 1916. New material, discovered in 1913 in the papers of Nicholas Biddle's grandsons.

Thwaites, Reuben Gold, ed. *Original Journals of the Lewis and Clark Expedition, 1804–1806.* 8 vols. New York: Dodd, Mead, 1904–5. Reprint, New York: Arno Press, 1969. A centennial birthday present—the first verbatim edition of all the known journals.

General

[Appleman, Roy E.]. *Lewis and Clark: Historic Places Associated with Their Transcontinental Exploration (1804–06).* The National Survey of Historic Sites and Buildings, ed. Robert G. Ferris, vol. 13. Washington, D.C.: Government Printing Office, 1975. Reprinted in paperback as Roy E. Appleman, *Lewis & Clark's Transcontinental Exploration, 1804–1806.* 3rd ed. Washington, D.C.: Jefferson National Expansion Historical Assoc., 2000. A good short narrative with excellent maps.

Fifer, Barbara, and Vicky Soderberg. *Along the Trail with Lewis and Clark.* Great Falls, Mont.: Montana Magazine, 1998. A tour guide, featuring excellent maps by Joseph Mussulman.

Jackson, Donald D., ed. *Letters of the Lewis and Clark Expedition with Related Documents, 1783–1854.* Urbana: University of Illinois Press, 1962; Reprint (in 2 vols.), 1978. An essential reference work.

Lavender, David. *The Way to the Western Sea: Lewis and Clark Across the Continent.* New York: Harper & Row, 1988. A good, general, comprehensive history.

Nasatir, A. P., ed. *Before Lewis and Clark: Documents Illustrating the History of the Missouri, 1785–1804.* 2 vols. St. Louis: St. Louis Historical Documents Foundation, 1952. Reprint, Lincoln: University of Nebraska Press, 1990. All that is known about the river and the west before 1804.

Schmidt, Thomas, *National Geographic's Guide to the Lewis and Clark Trail.* Washington, D.C.: National Geographic Society, 1998. A modern trail guide.

Wheeler, Olin D. *The Trail of Lewis and Clark, 1804–1806.* 2 vols. New York: G. P. Putnam's Sons, 1904. The author was a promotional writer for the Northern Pacific Railroad and Yellowstone National Park. The virtue of this trail guide is its age—it was written before dams and other developments obliterated most of the trail.

Biographies

Ambrose, Stephen E. *Undaunted Courage: Meriwether Lewis, Thomas Jefferson, and the Opening of the American West.* New York: Simon & Schuster, 1996. A stirring, patriotic biography; the book to read.

Bakeless, John. *Lewis and Clark: Partners in Discovery.* New York: William Morrow, 1947. Older and uncritical, but still the only treatment of Clark.

Betts, Robert B. *In Search of York: The Slave Who Went to the Pacific with Lewis and Clark.* Boulder: Colorado Associated University Press, 1985. Revised, Great Falls, Mont.: Lewis and Clark Trail Heritage Foundation, 2000. Beautifully illustrated summary of all that's known about York.

Clark, Ella E., and Margot Edmonds. *Sacagawea of the Lewis and Clark Expedition.* Berkeley: University of California Press, 1979. Another brief biography.

Clarke, Charles G. *The Men of the Lewis and Clark Expedition.* Glendale, Calif.: The Arthur H. Clark Co., 1970. Biographical sketches of all the principals.

Dillon, Richard. *Meriwether Lewis: A Biography.* New York: Coward-McCann, 1965. An older, romantic, heroic treatment.

Harris, Burton. *John Colter: His Years in the Rockies.* New York: Scribner, 1952. Reprint, Lincoln: University of Nebraska Press, 1993; Big Horn Book Co., Casper, Wyo., 1983. Colter's career as a fur trapper and explorer after Lewis and Clark.

Holmberg, James J., ed. *Dear Brother: Letters of William Clark to Jonathan Clark.* New Haven, Conn.: Yale University Press, 2002. Letters discovered in an attic in Louisville in 1988, with superb commentary.

Howard, Harold P. *Sacajawea.* Norman: University of Oklahoma Press, 1971. Standard biography.

Jackson, Donald D. *Thomas Jefferson and the Stony Mountains: Exploring the West from Monticello.* Urbana: University of Illinois Press, 1981. The full story of Jefferson's western interests; three pivotal chapters on Lewis and Clark.

Jenkinson, Clay. *The Character of Meriwether Lewis: "Completely Metamorphosed" in the American West*. Reno, Nev.: Marmouth Press, 2000. The best interpretation of Lewis's inability to publish and his suicide.

Kessler, Donna J. *The Making of Sacagawea: A Euro-American Legend*. Tuscaloosa: University of Alabama Press, 1996. How myths are made.

Ronda, James P. *Jefferson's West: A Journey with Lewis and Clark*. Monticello, Va.: Thomas Jefferson Foundation, 2000. Jefferson's hopes and western realities.

Steffen, Jerome O. *William Clark: Jeffersonian Man on the Frontier*. Norman: University of Oklahoma Press, 1977. Clark's post-Expedition career.

Science

Allen, John Logan. *Passage through the Garden: Lewis and Clark and the Image of the American Northwest*. Urbana,: University of Illinois Press, 1975. Reprint, Dover Publications, 1991. A groundbreaking geographical study.

Botkin, Daniel B. *Our Natural History: The Lessons of Lewis and Clark*. New York: Putnam, 1995. Connections between the natural history of Lewis and Clark and current concerns.

Burroughs, Raymond Darwin, ed. *The Natural History of the Lewis and Clark Expedition*. East Lansing: Michigan State University Press, 1961. Selections from the *Journals*.

Chuinard, Eldon G. *Only One Man Died: The Medical Aspects of the Lewis & Clark Expedition*. Glendale, Calif.: A. H. Clark Co., 1979. The author, an osteopath, lovingly recounts infirmities.

Cutright, Paul Russell. *Lewis and Clark: Pioneering Naturalists*. Urbana: University of Illinois Press, 1969. Absolutely essential study of scientific discoveries.

Plamondon, II, Martin. *Lewis and Clark Trail Maps: A Cartographic Reconstruction*. 2 vols. Pullman: Washington State University Press, 2000. The best modern depictions.

Ronda, James P. *Lewis and Clark among the Indians*. Lincoln: University of Nebraska Press, 1984. Ethnological account that emphasizes the contributions of Native Americans to the success of the Expedition.

Other

Eide, Ingvard Henry. *American Odyssey: The Journey of Lewis and Clark*. Chicago: Rand McNally, 1969. The best photographic album.

Fisher, Vardis. *Tale of Valor: A Novel of the Lewis and Clark Expedition*. Garden City, N.Y.: Doubleday, 1958. The best novel.

Furtwangler, Albert. *Acts of Discovery: Visions of America in the Lewis and Clark Journals.* Urbana: University of Illinois Press, 1993. Imaginative and philosophical journal readings.

Gillette, Lance. "Bibliography of the Lewis and Clark Expedition." http://www.olypen.com/gillde/lance/bibliographies/lewis.htm. Books, chapters, articles, and annotation.

Jackson, Donald. *Among the Sleeping Giants: Occasional Pieces on Lewis and Clark.* Urbana: University of Illinois Press, 1987. Essays by a premier Expedition scholar.

Lewis and Clark: The Journey of The Corps of Discovery. Produced by Dayton Duncan and Ken Burns. 240 min. Florentine Films and WETA-TV, 1997. Videocassette.

Ronda, James P., ed. *Finding the West: Explorations with Lewis and Clark.* Albuquerque: University of New Mexico Press, 2001. An anthology of seven essays.

————. *Voyages of Discovery: Essays on the Lewis and Clark Expedition.* Helena: Montana Historical Society Press, 1998. Articles and commentary.

VIAs, Inc. *Discovering Lewis and Clark.* http://www.lewis-clark.org. An interactive web site.

We Proceeded On. The official publication of the Lewis and Clark Trail Heritage Foundation, Inc. Quarterly. 27 vols., to date, 1974-present. $30 per year. Write: Membership Coordinator, The Lewis and Clark Trail Heritage Foundation, Inc., PO Box 3434, Great Falls, MT 59403.

INDEX

About the Author

HARRY WILLIAM FRITZ is Professor and Chair of the Department of History at the University of Montana, Missoula.